other books by Ray Miller:

Vol. 1 FROM HERE TO OBSCURITY   Model T Fords
Vol. 2 HENRY'S LADY   Model A Fords
Vol. 3 THE V-8 AFFAIR   Early V-8 Fords
Vol. 4 THUNDERBIRD!   Ford's T-Bird
Vol. 5 NIFTY FIFTIES Fords   Post-War V-8 Fords
Vol. 6 MUSTANG Does It!   Ford's Mustang
Vol. 7 FALCON!   The New-Size Ford

Vol. 1 CHEVROLET: Coming of Age   1911-1942 Chevrolets
Vol. 2 CHEVROLET: USA #1   1946-1959 Chevrolets
Vol. 3 The Real CORVETTE   Chevrolet's Sports Car
Vol. 4 CAMARO!   Chevy's Classy Chassis

The Evergreen Press
Oceanside, California

FALCON!

the New-Size Ford

By RAY MILLER

FALCON!

the New-Size Ford

First Printing
1982

Library of Congress Catalog Card #82-090194
ISBN 0-913056-11-1

Printed by:
    Sierra Printers, Inc.
    Bakersfield, California

Typesetting by:
    Lockwood Litho
    Oceanside, California

Photo Processing by:
    KJM Photo/Graphics
    Sebastopol, California

Printed in the U.S.A.

The Evergreen Press
Box 1711
Oceanside, CA 92054

RAY MILLER, an Oceanside, California, resident for almost 15 years, has devoted himself to providing an unusual series (actually *two* series) of books in which specific cars are covered in photographic detail never before attempted. Described variously as "an absolute must", "for fans who like to look at old cars", "Top quality photographic reporting", his books have received an unmatched acceptance.

Beginning in 1971 with the publication of FROM HERE TO OBSCURITY which he co-authored with Bruce McCalley, editor of *THE VINTAGE FORD*, his efforts picked up speed as he produced HENRY'S LADY and THE V-8 AFFAIR which dealt with the pre-war Fords. Then came THUNDER-BIRD!, followed shortly by the Real CORVETTE, NIFTY-FIFTIES Fords, and the two-volume in-depth study CHEV-ROLET: Coming of Age, and CHEVROLET: USA #1. MUS-TANG Does It! was next, then CAMARO! Chevy's *Classy* Chassis, and he now turns his attention to FALCON! Ford's New-Size Car.

This book brings to seven the number of volumes in the highly regarded FORD ROAD SERIES, and provides the reader with a unique opportunity to note the similarities as *well* as the differences between adjacent car lines.

RAY has been interested in cars for many years, having owned and driven both Ford and Chevrolet products and an occasional Chrysler. With characteristic enthusiasm, his approach to these books encourages his purchase and restoration of subject vehicles. In this case, he has enlarged his Collection with the addition of a beautifully restored 1965 Ranchero.

Southern California is particularly well adapted to works of this type. With the excellent year-round weather, automobiles do not suffer the destruction by the elements to the degree that they do elsewhere. Thus, many fine cars remain in service for far longer periods and can be seen daily on the Freeways. From this source are selected those cars which are used for illustrative models. It is RAY MILLER'S exceptional skill in making appropriate determinations that enable a reference book such as this to be produced.

THE EVERGREEN PRESS
Oceanside, California 92054

The Author wishes to thank those who contributed much of their time and their interest towards making this a better book than it might otherwise have become.

The Owners, generally mentioned by name within the text of this book are again thanked. Their patient understanding of the needs of the photographer and their willingness to share their own special discoveries with him have advanced the cause. Their patience in allowing us to crawl over, under, and through, their automobiles has permitted us to present these unique views.

WOODROW HAINES and Members of the Ford Division Public Relations Staff provided information, photographs, and above all, encouragement.

CHRIS CARROLL of Antique Automobile of San Diego opened his inventory of parts to our camera and enabled us to present many details more clearly.

BILL ANDERSON displayed an enthusiasm unmatched when he agreed to repaint his 1960 two-door sedan to provide a better model.

BILL BAILEY of Royal Oak, Michigan, voluntarily furnished much needed aid in the form of early photos, documents, and similar material.

GARY HUCKINS, current President of the Falcon Club of San Diego, furnished the names and addresses of many owners of cars which qualified for study, and encouraged the Members' support of the project.

ROY SWORD, President of the Falcon Club of America lighted the way for it all by establishing his Club as a Source before the collection and restoration of the Falcons was at all a fashionable or acceptable hobby.

KEN OVERMILLER, founder and first President of the Falcon Club of San Diego received this project with enthusiasm and spent much time in encouraging and educating the Author.

JACK MILLER, of Hollywood, California, Falcon parts supplier, found and supplied many unusual items.

TOM McRAE, Service Manager of Dixon Ford in Carlsbad provided many early Catalogs and other needed literature.

HAROLD CARPENTER, of Oceanside, located and supplied for photographs many of the rare wheel covers seen on page 294 and following.

MIKE and KATHY JACKSON of Spring Valley were so very pleasant; when it became necessary to make not two, but four attempts to shoot the dust jacket photograph, they merely smiled, then cleaned and re-polished their beautiful 1965 Convertible.

To these, and to the far greater number whose names may not appear in these pages, we again express our gratitude for their interst, their help, and their encouragement. This book is a better effort for their help.

rjm

6

During the 1950's, American cars were caught up in a competitive growth in size. As each successive model appeared, it resembled the previous one, but never was it smaller, shorter, or lighter. Perception of the American public was trained in the "bigger is better" school and this perception was enforced by the domestic manufacturers as Ford, typical of the Industry, saw its full-size car grow over 18 inches in length to a hefty 17.8 feet overall!

Imported cars however were generally smaller; as an example, the popular Volkswagen sedan was shorter by almost five feet! Traditional "comforts" were lacking in many imports, but a significant part of Detroit's market was becoming receptive to the smaller, lighter, "more economical" cars. U.S. Imports climbed to close to ten per cent of 1959 model year production and the American Motors Corporation's little Rambler was selling well; by 1959 it was filling some 6.7% of the domestic total and growing rapidly.

Ford was certainly not alone in perceiving the enlarging market segment, but Ford *was* the first of the three major manufacturers to bring to the marketplace a car designed specifically to fill new requirements for a smaller, lighter, more fuel-efficient, more comfortable, and more crisply styled car. So new was this entrant that it was described merely as the "New-Size Car"!

Introduced on October 8, 1959, the Falcon was offered as *transportation*. Unlike the Mustang which was later derived from it, Falcon was offered with a very narrow choice of Options. Intended as inexpensive transportation, it claimed "up to 30 miles per gallon on regular gas"! It provided room for six passengers (against 4 for most imports) and was the result of a three year and three-million mile development and test program.

No wonder the early Falcon was so well received! In the 12 months following its introduction, over half a million were produced, and by the end of its second model year almost *one million* Falcons had been manufactured, a record that would be exceeded only by that of the derivative Mustang in the mid-Sixties. Falcon had most certainly hit its intended mark.

With the 1963 addition of a Convertible and then the Sprint Convertible and Hardtop in mid-year, the Falcon sought to capture a "sporty" image to gloss the fading "Economy Car" label, and by skillful restyling, the 1964 and 1965 models certainly attained that goal. The wisdom of abandoning the Marque and substituting a newly-named totally re-styled line was confirmed when the new Mustang, introduced in mid-1964 surpassed its parent and went on to still higher achievements in production, while the Falcon would slowly but surely wind down as a conservative, somewhat plainly styled, offering. Finally eliminated in 1970, the Falcon nevertheless had its moments and is presented here with enthusiasm for what it was and what it might have been.

rjm

ABC's OF THE

Ford Falcon

. . . THE NEW-SIZE FORD

EASIEST CAR IN THE WORLD TO OWN

TWO AUTO MAKERS
PICK SAME NAMES

But Ford wins Falcon Only
Minutes Over Chrysler

The Ford Motor Company won a close race with coincidence.

Both Ford and the Chrysler Corporation, unknown to each other, chose the name Falcon for their new small cars. But because Ford reserved the name with an industry registry only twenty minutes ahead of Chrysler, it won the right to the name.

Ford and Chrysler independently settled on Falcon, but Ford won by notifying the Automobile Manufactures Association of its choice twenty minutes ahead of Chrysler. The association is the official industry arbiter and its Proprietary Name File is the trade-name bible for the car makers.

Actually Chrysler was said to have been the first to indicate its interest in the name Falcon, when it asked that a search be made on the availability of the name.

The report was made, but while the Company was making its final decision, Ford called and registered the name, unaware, association officials said, that Chrysler was considering it too.

Falcon is not new to the automobile industry. The roster of 2600 names that have graced the automotive scene in the last sixty years shows that Falcon was used by two other manufactures. A Falcon passenger car was made in 1922 and a Falcon-Knight was marketed in 1926.

Industry sources noted that it was possible although not likely, for Chrysler and General Motors to shift to other names for their new cars. Ford however appears firmly decided on Falcon.

New York Times 5/21/59
© New York Times. Reprinted By Permission

Twenty Minutes! One third of an hour. A microcosm in automotive history. That's all that it was though; just twenty minutes and an entirely different name would have had to be applied to Ford's new product!

A Ford executive acted decisively and made the selection. Thus he earned a continuing honor. The name "Falcon" continued on to bring him pride.

It was his subordinate however, who responded immediately to his instructions. By ignoring natural tendencies to procrastinate, and even (probably) foregoing a morning coffee-break, he managed to report Ford's choice barely in time to secure the name!

To that unknown Ford employee, we happily dedicate this book.

Table of Contents

Front End Recognition.................................12

Introduction..14

Typical Falcon Advertisments..........................20

1960 "The New-Size Ford".............................26

1961 "The World's Most Successful New Car"............50

1962 "Best Shape Economy's Ever Been In"..............70

1963 "Now with V-8's"................................94

1964 "The Total Performance Compact".................144

1965 "Total Performance Falcons".....................204

1966 "America's Economy Champ with a new Sporty Look".......266

1967 "Better Idea in Economy".......................274

1968 "Another Better Idea from Ford"................282

1969 "Big Car Idea . . . Small Car Price"...........288

1970 "The One for the Money"........................290

1970½ "All-New Edition"............................293

Wheels & Wheelcovers...............................294

Some Typical Assessories...........................301

Decoding the Data Plate............................316

Production Statistics..............................318

1960 Falcon & Ranchero

1961 Falcon & Ranchero

1962 Falcon & Ranchero

1963 Falcon & Ranchero

1964 Falcon & Ranchero

1965 Falcon & Ranchero

1966 Falcon

1966 Ford Ranchero

1967 Falcon

1967 Fairlane Ranchero

1968-70 Falcon

1968-69 Fairlane Ranchero

In retrospect it _was_ a superb idea! Just build a car that would comfortably seat six adults; would have power to spare, especially on acceleration; would sell for the price of an economy Import; would be servicable at any of over 4000 local Dealerships; and would provide a reliable fuel economy of over 30 miles per gallon!

Falcon _was_ all of that and more! It's _only_ problem was, sadly, that it was twenty years ahead of its time.

Almost unnoticed, in the 1950's small, undersized by U.S. standards, under-powered by the same standards, and remarkably unstyled automobiles started to flow into this country from Germany, France, and Japan. Ignored by virtually all, these early imported cars were slowly but steadily to impact on the Industry with devastating effect.

Without doubt the most popular, Volkswagen's strange-looking Beetle became the import Leader, and the feisty little "bug" could be seen on our Freeways running with all-out abandon as it wove abruptly between the larger, and less agile, Detroit-built automobiles. When, in 1958, Volkswagen German-built imported car sales reached to over 100,000 units, it was time to act to meet this challenge and the Ford Motor Company was thus to place in production their "New-Size" car. Earlier, Ford was not above "playing games", for as late as February 19, 1957,

1960 Falcon 4-Door Sedan

closed-circuit TV News Conference. What they saw was the New Size 1960 Ford Falcon, a car that would today be described as a "down-sized" Ford. It had the things that the Imports did not. It had style, riding comfort, room for six adults, and, above all, a Service Network of over 4000 Dealers.

On October 8, 1959, Ford Dealers all over the country were able to show and demonstrate the Falcon. Public acceptance confirmed Ford's concept; the American Public _was_ ready to "economize". In its first year, over 435,000 units were to be produced, a new record for first-year sales, and in 1961, almost 500,000 more would be built. Only the derivitive Mustang in 1965 would exceed this achievement.

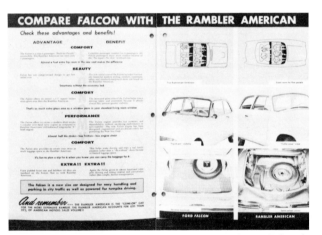

Ford perceived the American Motors Rambler as Falcon's domestic competition and provided their Dealers with this detailed comparison.

the President of Ford refused to confirm that the car was coming. However, by May, it was an open secret and both Ford and Chrysler annouced plans to build a new small car. General Motors responded almost immediately with an announcement of their own new Corvair and the race was on.

In 1958, Ford had introduced a new car aimed at the specific Market that lay between their Mercury and Lincoln lines. Generally seen as a competitor for GM's Buick, the Edsel was to become one of the world's outstanding blunders and when it was suspended in its 1960 model year had cost Ford an awesome sum. Despite their loss, Ford's Management Team approved the "New-Size" Ford and proceeded with its development, an action that has to be seen in this light to be fully appreciated.

On September 21, 1959, the Ford Motor Company, in an unprecedented event, unveiled its new Falcon to newsmen throughout the country in a

On September 25, 1959, Ford revealed the new 1960 full-size models. These were described as "the longest, widest, and lowest in the Company's history". Just three weeks earlier, the Falcon has been enthusiastically described as being "nearly three feet shorter; 1000 pounds lighter, than the standard Fords". Ford was obviously hedging their bet and seeking to accommodate both extremes.

Initially Falcon was to be an unembellished basic car. Only a 2-Door and a 4-Door Sedan were offered and the upgrading Options were limited. By January though, the Station Wagon and Ranchero were added to the line and choice was widened. Of a fairly large number of available Options, perhaps the most significant was Fordomatic, an automatic transmission. A surprise in view of the public's perception of the manual VW floor shift as "sporty" was Ford's failure to offer a floor-mounted transmission shift of any type.

For 1961, a new optional engine appeared, providing 101 horsepower in place of the standard 85 HP Falcon SIX. In addition to a new Sedan Delivery, Falcon also introduced a Deluxe Body Side Trim available along with its earlier side window dress-up trim for a new emphasis on "Deluxe" as a sales aid. Little else changed though in this second year

The 1961 Falcon featured a new convex aluminum grille and offered an optional 101 horsepower engine.

14

New models included the Squire Wagon, a luxury version of the Falcon wagon with wood-grained exterior trim, a new Station Bus and Club Wagon built, surprisingly, on a 90" wheelbase (against 109.5" for the passenger cars), and the Futura, an upgraded two-door sedan with standard bucket seats and a center console.

In February, the 1962 Falcon line was again revised, this time by the addition of a Futura Sports Sedan, a "lively and luxurious" new model with a roofline based on Thunderbird styling, replacing the early-year Futura.

1963 saw the emergence of "Futura" as the upper line of Falcon Sedans as both a Futura 2-Door and 4-Door appeared, but 1963's big news was the introduction of the Futura Convertible (with bench seats) and the Futura Sports Convertible (with bucket seats) followed shortly by the Sprint Convertible with the Falcon 170 Special SIX engine, bucket seats, tachometer, and 4-speed manual transmission all standard.

In January of 1963, the addition of the Fairlane 260 cu. in. engine as a Falcon option was announced as part of the Company's 1963½ Product Line. This engine became standard in the Sprint Hardtop

Instrument Panel of the 1960 Ford Falcon. From an Evaluation Report by General Motors Proving Ground, dated 9-22-59, over two weeks prior to the public introduction on October 8th.

of Falcon's existence as almost one million of the New-Size Fords were placed on America's roads.

Seen by many as entirely too archaic, the rounded lines of the 1960-61 Falcons were to be supplanted with a transitional design in 1962. Lines of these cars were less rounded and served as a continuing concept through 1963 to be followed in 1964 by a far more angular body which may have represented the high point of development of a unique Falcon styling.

1962 brought with it to the Falcon line some new Styling, some new models, new luxury interior choices, new fuel and oil savings in improved versions of the Falcon SIX, and some new all-around economies including a new 30,000 mile radiator coolant.

BOLTED-ON FRONT FENDERS

A feature of the new Falcon was the bolted-on front fender. Although Ford had been using this approach since 1908, "bolted-on front fenders" became a Falcon advertising claim.

and Convertible replacing the big SIX and rendering those earlier six-cylinder Sprints rare indeed.

1964 Falcons seemed larger than earlier models but most of the increased size was illusory. Overall length had increased only one half inch, and width was up by one inch, but most of the change in appearance was due to the straighter lines which typified the new cars.

Still advertising the results of the Mobil Los Angeles-to-Chicago Economy Run which was won in 1962 by the Falcon with over 32 mph, Falcon nevertheless offered a new 200 cubic inch SIX in addition to the four engines offered in 1963. Little was changed in the model lineup as the Sprint Convertible and Hardtop was still at the top of the line, followed by the Futura versions of the same body styles. Futura Sedans led Falcon Sedans and the Squire Wagon was followed by Falcon 2-door and 4-door Wagons.

Ranchero offered both a Standard and a Deluxe bench seat version and a Deluxe Ranchero with standard bucket seats. An optional Futura-style

The 1960 Falcon introduced "Single-Unit Design", a frameless unibody construction with a vibration isolated sub-frame to carry the engine and transmission. This highly successful design was carried forward into other lines, not the least of which was the Mustang in 1964.

FORD RANCHERO FACTS

- Max. GVW 4600 lbs. (½ Ton Pickup).
- Max. payload capacity 1190 lbs.
- Pickup box capacity 30.4 cu. ft.
- Choice of 3 transmissions; 3-speed conventional standard; optional 3-speed overdrive or Fordomatic.
- 7.50 x 14-4 p.r. tubeless tires Std. with

- 5½" safety type rims; Max. tires 8.0 x 14-6 p.r.
- Total brake lining area 191.4 sq. in. (suspended brake pedal).
- Ranchero offers—144 H.P. 223 Six or 190 H.P. 272 V-8; Custom Ranchero 144 H.P. 223 Six or 212 H.P. 292 V-8.

FEATURES

- Smart Passenger car styling, riding comfort, and handling ease.
- Standard full width rear window, biggest of any pickup in the industry.
- Sturdy pickup body construction with double steel floor for extra strength and durability.

- Famous Ford 4-Way Ball Joint front suspension, plus front and rear shocks for easiest ride.
- Body sides scarcely 3 feet above ground for easiest loading or unloading.
- Choice of 11 attractive colors, a total of 5 interior trim combinations offered.

For 1957 and Years Ahead – FORD TRUCKS Cost Less –
Less to own . . . Less to run . . . Last Longer, Too!

The 1960 Ranchero was not Ford's first. Ranchero had been introduced in the 1957 line, but through 1959 it was a "Full-Size" vehicle.

dual Body Side Stripe with rear fender ornaments was available for any model. The Sedan Delivery continued to be offered in both Standard and Deluxe versions, and the Club Wagons were unchanged.

> "Hey, Boss, these Falcons are thought to be an 'old man's car'. All that they offer is style and economy. After all, there is a younger segment of the Market out there that really resists identifying with the stodgy Falcon."

> "Let's take the Falcon, shorten the rear deck, lengthen the hood, make bucket seats standard, use as many Falcon parts as possible, add about a hundred Available Options, and give it a new name."

The Falcon's best known derivitive, the Ford Mustang, was thus introduced in April as a 1964½ model and would sell over 500,000 in

The new Falcon Ranchero was introduced to the Dealers in March of 1960 with this Special Product & Merchandising Bulletin.

its first 12 month, reaching a total of over one million in less than 24 months of production. Although the 1965 Falcon would go well over 200,000 units, its days were numbered.

1965 saw the new 289 cu. in. V-8 option replace both the Challenger and the Sprint versions of earlier 260 V-8. Sprint became a less meaningful package and was now merely an emblem-and-bucket seat addition to the Convertibles and the Hardtops. The intermediate Futura Sports Coupe and Sprots Convertible were dropped although bucket seats were available in Futura Hardtops and Convertible.

The 1965 Ranchero offered a Standard and a Deluxe bench seat model plus a Standard and a Deluxe bucket-seat version. Deluxe bucket seat models had

The 1960 Ranchero Sales Folder was that vehicle's most attractive. Featuring 12 pages, including unique cut-outs, it was a heavily illustrated 4-color booklet.

At the same time, Ford announced the new Falcon Club Wagons and Station Bus. Shown here is the Deluxe Club Wagon which is designed to carry eight passengers, or easily convert to a camping unit, mobile home, or all-around utility cargo vehicle.

The new 1962 Squire Wagon was introduced on September 19, 1961. The "Dressed-up" luxury wagon had a simulated wood exterior trim with dark horizontal emphasis lines to suggest planking and distinctive chromed rear quarter trim strips.

The Falcon Sports Futura, announced on February 14, 1962, featured a Thunderbird-like roofline, bucket seats, and an optional floor-mounted 4-Speed manual transmission.

The popular Futura Convertible was first available in the new 1963 Falcon line. Offered with bench or with bucket seats, over 30,000 were produced in addition to almost 5000 Sprint Convertibles introduced later in the model year.

Falcon's image improved when this red, white, and blue 1962 Falcon finished second in its class at the gruelling 12-Hour Grand Prix of Endurance Race at Sebring on March 24, 1962. Race-prepared by Holman-Moody, the car was powered by a highly tuned Ford Fairlane 260 cu. in. V-8 engine.

This unique paint scheme, featuring a white (red on white cars) side stripe and cab roof together with 1964-style Body Side Trim, was offered only on the 1965 Ranchero.

The 1966 Falcon was presented on 9/21/65. With its new long hood, short rear deck, rear quarter "hop-up" and round wheel openings, the car was offered as an alternative to the similar Mustang.

standard bright rocker panel moldings and a Body Side Molding consisting of a single stripe. Optional was a two-tone paint that employed the 1964 dual Body Side Trim as parting line emphasis.

The Sedan Delivery was offered only in its Standard version, and the Squire Wagon, offered in 1965 for the last time, was followed by the Futura and the Falcon 2-door and 4-door Wagons.

1965 was to be the last year of aggressive Marketing for the Falcon line and marked the end of the line's most interesting period.

The 1966 and following Falcons were limited to 2-door and 4-door models including the Hardtops, Con-

1967 Falcon had distinctive simulated vents on front fenders. Select-Shift Cruise-O-Matic allowing manual or automatic shifting appeared as a new Option.

1968 Falcon introduced a radiator grille that would survive unchanged to January 1, 1970.

vertibles, and Squire having been dropped. Even the Ranchero was to be wrested from the Falcon line and would reappear in 1967 as a Fairlane. Little would then change from 1968 to early 1970 as cosmetic changes of little significance and data plate numerical revisions seemed to constitute Falcon's progress.

The end of the true Falcon came with the end of the 1965 production, but a further interesting event was the termination of Falcon production entirely on January 1, 1970. For a brief time thereafter, the "1970½" Falcon was offered. In reality, this car was a Torino 2-door or 4-door bearing Falcon left-over nameplates.

With this action the final ignominy occurred. Falcon's demise had come partly because of its identification as an "economy" car, but the 1970½ Falcon/Torino was offered with seven engine choices up to an awesome 370 horsepower 429 cu. in. Cobra Jet Ram-Air V-8! Little wonder that this misidentified effort was to be shortly eliminated from Ford's offerings.

1969 Falcon, essentially unchanged from 1968, continued to offer the smart Sports Coupe, an upgraded 2-Door car.

A large Promotional Budget was assigned to Falcon at its inception and the results were saturation advertising. Initially stressing Economy, early ads often pointed out the added benefits of the Falcon over other domestic and imported "economy cars". Among these were Comfort, Style, and Performance, claims that were really not far from the truth.

The first official facts about

Ford Falcon

A statement by Henry Ford II

I doubt if there's ever been a new car more talked about, rumored about and guessed about than the new Ford Falcon . . . the New-size Ford. In describing the Falcon to you, it is perhaps easier to begin with what it is not.

It is not just a small car. It is not just a smaller Ford. It is not just an economy car. It is not the kind of car that's dangerous to take out on a great modern turnpike, in the midst of heavy truck-and-trailer traffic.

It is a beautifully sophisticated new kind of Ford that combines low cost and great economy with beautiful styling, superb comfort and complete resources of power and safety.

When you look the Falcon over in your Ford Dealer's showroom, please keep one important fact in mind: the Falcon is in no way an experimental car. All of its

engineering principles are the proven, best way of building a car. Three full years of planning, building, testing and refining have gone into the Falcon. It is a carefully thought out, carefully checked out car.

Nor does the Ford Motor Company come to the economy car field as a stranger. We have built millions of such cars in our overseas plants. We have learned a lot about economy cars from these operations. We have learned a lot about American car needs from the 50 million Fords built in this country.

In the Falcon we have summed up all this experience in producing a U.S.-built economy car, specifically designed for U.S. driving conditions.

It was my hope that we could find some way of proving the Falcon's greatness to you before the car came out. Not in terms of a test—for the Falcon passed and repassed every test we could devise long ago. We needed some way of showing you —no matter what kind of driving you experience in your part of the country— the Falcon can fill all your car needs, beautifully, comfortably, safely and economically.

We found the way in Experience Run, U.S.A. The first Falcons off the production line were sent on a trip covering every last mile of numbered Federal Highways in the country. This is the longest, most thorough proving ever given a new car in America. In order to cover such a tremendous mileage in just 22 days, cars had to be run "around the clock."

Experience Run, U.S.A. was a dramatic, public demonstration of facts our engineers had already proved on the Ford test tracks. During the later stages of our track testing, Falcons were driven even more miles than the Experience Run, U.S.A. total . . . so we knew what this car could do! And Experience Run, U.S.A. is proof for all to see . . . proof right on your highways, your city streets.

The hundreds of thousands of miles these cars have traveled on our test tracks and during Experience Run, U.S.A. combine to make the Ford Falcon the world's most experienced new car!

Henry Ford

Following is a series of questions and answers on the New-size Ford. They are now available in booklet form at your Ford Dealer's.

How about gas mileage?

The Falcon's Experience Run U.S.A. is the best proof of that. The drivers' own mile-by-mile log books show that the Falcons averaged over 30 M.P.G. in all kinds of driving . . . including city traffic, mountain climbing . . . everything American roads have to offer.

What can the average Falcon owner expect?

More than 50% better gas mileage than from an average, low-priced American car.

It is reported that the Falcon is 181 inches long. Is this true—and if so— how does this compare with the size of a Ford Galaxie?

The Falcon is exactly 181.2 inches long. Its wheelbase is 109.5 inches. To picture 181 inches, look at a new Ford Falcon against the outline of a new 1960 Ford Galaxie.

Another way of putting it: the average full-sized American car measures 215-220 inches. However, even these simple comparisons don't give a true picture of the Falcon's new size. For the Falcon actually has **two** new sizes . . . an outside size **and** inside size.

What's the difference?

Quite a bit! Outside, the Falcon is sized to give all the handling and parking advantages of a smaller car. But inside, the Falcon is really a big car.

How many people can it seat?

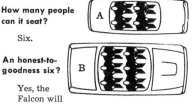

Six.

An honest-to-goodness six?

Yes, the Falcon will seat six big adults in perfect comfort . . . with their feet outstretched, their shoulders held naturally, hands by their sides and hats on their heads. As you can see, above, the foreign cars (A) seat four comfortably . . . the Falcon (B) seats six big adults in **even greater comfort.**

This well constructed early two-page advertisement appeared late in 1959 at the introduction of the Falcon. In it were presented facts about the new car along with a Statement by Ford's then-President Henry Ford II.

the new size Ford for 1960

How much luggage space does the Falcon have?

There's over 3 times more luggage space in the Falcon than in the most popular foreign import . . . 23 cubic feet in all.

How much luggage will that 23 cubic feet accommodate?

That's room for 2 men's two-suiters, a lady's wardrobe, a lady's overnight case, a lady's train case, a man's overnight case and a set of golf clubs.

There are many more Falcon luxury-car comforts never before seen in a car this size, at this price.

Such as?

Such as foam-padded seating, arm rests, a Lifeguard Steering Wheel, Lifeguard Double-Grip Door Locks, door checks that hold the doors open, a heavy-duty battery, elegant new nylon fabrics that stay cleaner longer. Standard 3-speed transmission has American shift pattern—nothing new to learn. Then, too, there's a new Fordomatic transmission for easy, American-style, no-shift driving. Full U.S.-style instrument panel to keep the driver informed of fuel, oil, electric system. Far, far greater visibility, too. The Falcon has 3,732 square inches of total glass area—almost double the glass area in the most popular imported economy cars—even **more** than some full-size 1959 American sedans. And, for your all-year-round comfort, the Falcon has one of the finest heater-ventilation systems in the industry.

Let's get back to gas mileage for a moment.

Certainly.

Aside from gas mileage, is the Falcon an economy car?

If by economy car you mean one that saves you substantial money—it certainly is!

Do the facts back that up?

Well, the Falcon goes 4,000 miles between oil changes. Its Diamond Lustre Finish never needs waxing. Then, too, power brakes and power steering—two popular extra-cost options—are unnecessary in the Falcon. In fact, they're not available. Remember—there's almost a ton less car to stop and steer. Insurance and maintenance should cost less in a Falcon, too.

Why should insurance and maintenance cost less?

Much easier servicing. For example, an entire fender can be replaced in minutes for only a few dollars. Every part of the Falcon has been engineered for just this sort of quicker, lower cost servicing **anywhere.**

Anywhere?

Over 6,900 Ford Dealers across the country will offer **complete** Falcon care.

Honestly now—will owners feel safe and secure driving the Falcon on our modern superhighways?

That sounds like a comparison of the Falcon with the foreign economy cars.

Is such a comparison valid?

No! Such a comparison just couldn't be further from the truth. The Falcon has been specifically designed for U.S.A. super-highway travel—with more than **twice** the power of the most popular foreign imports. There is no highway anywhere in America where a driver has to be afraid of taking the Falcon. The best proof of this is the Falcon's Experience Run U.S.A. . . . over every mile of numbered Federal Highways in the country.

Just how fast can the Falcon go?

Most drivers will never get the chance to see. Ford test drivers were honestly amazed by the Falcon's nonchalance in pulling out and passing some highly touted American "powerhouses." On the 60-70 mph turnpikes, it cruised **all day** like a big car. There's no doubt about the Falcon's "big-car" performance. Its all-new, six-cylinder engine was specifically designed to power the Falcon's new weight and new size . . . and in no way is this new engine a rework or adaptation of Ford's famous Mileage Maker Six.

Where is the Falcon's engine located . . . front or rear?

Up front—where most engineers and owners believe it belongs.

Why should a front-mounted engine be preferred?

This is a hard question, so let's start at the beginning. There are 3 different engine locations that can be used on a car. One is the rear-mounted engine.

In this type layout the engine is in the back and the luggage space up front. This design has become very popular in many of the small, post-war foreign imports.

The second possibility is front-engine design with front-wheel drive.

Here everything is centered up front . . . with engine power applied directly to the

front wheels. This design has not proved to be practical.

Third, is the conventional front-engine design with engine power transmitted to the rear wheels through a driveshaft.

This design—which is used for the Falcon—has been by far the most successful. Its **dependability has been proven in over 200 million cars.** With the engine up front, the car's center of gravity is forward for better directional stability. This gives the driver more positive, easier control of the car.

People often say: the bigger the car, the smoother the ride. Where does that leave the Falcon?

The Falcon is out front in riding comfort . . . because up front the Falcon will have the same famous Ball-Joint suspension as all 1960 Fords. Only the coil springs have been mounted differently to give the Falcon a steadier, more stable, "longer wheelbase" ride. Special built-in rebound controls in the front shock absorbers allow the Falcon to soak up road shock just as effectively as cars weighing 1,000 pounds more.

Is there any truth in the report the Falcon does not have a frame?

The report is true. It refers to the Falcon's new unitized body. This method of construction does away with a car's frame as it is known today. The frame is now an integral part of the body structure.

Is there any particular advantage in this unitized body?

In the Falcon, unitized construction makes it possible to build a car of minimum size and weight—yet with maximum strength, safety, comfort and freedom from rattles. While on the subject of body construction, here's another important point. All vital Falcon body areas are of a new galvanized steel that helps prevent rust. This new steel process is still a Ford secret.

One last question. What's the styling concept behind this car?

Very simply stated—an economy car doesn't need to have an economy-car look. That's why the Falcon has a marked resemblance to the entire 1960 Ford line . . . including the most luxurious models. The Falcon is the newest evidence that Ford builds the world's most beautifully proportioned cars.

FORD DIVISION,

TYPICAL FALCON ADVERTISEMENTS

This 1960 ad stressed the family-oriented design of the New-Size Falcon. Even a large pet dog was included, subtly to suggest roominess.

1960 Ranchero ad stressed its position as the "lowest priced pickup truck".

This 1961 ad neglected to refer to it as a "Ranchero", calling it the "Ford Falcon Pickup" instead.

EVERY WEEK 10,000 PEOPLE BOUNCE ON ITS SEATS, HONK ITS HORN, KICK ITS TIRES, SLAM ITS DOORS, SHOP AROUND___ DICKER, DICKER, DICKER___ AND THEN BUY THIS CAR!

Another 1960 ad capitalized on the interest that Falcon was generating at Dealer's showrooms.

With its wide public acceptance, Falcon was to have the best first-year sales of any new car to date. Ford did not lose the opportunity to advertise this fact.

OVER 550,000 PEOPLE ALREADY OWN THIS CAR

could it be they know something you don't?

By 1961, the numbers had reached well over a half-million and Falcon's advertisements made certain to so note the fact.

23

TYPICAL FALCON ADVERTISEMENTS

Starting in 1961, and for a large portion of 1962, the popular "Peanuts" characters, including Charlie Brown, Lucy, and of course, Snoopy, were employed in Falcon advertisements. They were dropped in mid-1962 with the introduction of the more sophisticated Sports Futura model.

In 1961, as more competing compacts were announced, Falcon continued to make favorable comparisons.

The bigger the compact car field gets...

...the better Falcon looks!

The Falcon's fuel economy was unbelieveable. In the Mobilgas Los Angeles-to-Chicago Economy run, Falcon lead its field with an incredible 32.6 miles per gallon!

1st and 2nd place Mobilgas Economy Run Drivers...
...reveal their secrets

Following up, this 1961 ad noted that Falcons won both first and second place, and divulged economy driving secrets.

New models for 1962 included the Squire Wagon and Club Wagons. These were included in this early-year ad.

With the 1963 introduction of a Falcon Convertible, an attempt was made to upgrade the line and for the first time, an ad tied the car to the luxurious top-of-the-line Thunderbird.

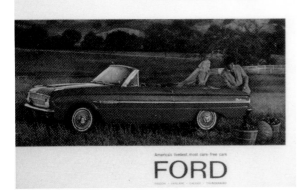

By March of 1963, the new 1962 Sports Futura appeared and was noted in greatly modernized ads such as this.

25

Stressing the new Convertible and Squire Wagon along with the Sports Futura, this 1963 Falcon ad now sold "Fun" tied to the "economy champ".

Falcons were entered in the grueling Monte Carlo Rallye and acquited themselves creditably. Results of the campaign were published in this 1964 ad.

Amazing new money-saving device
– the 1965 Falcon!

Falcon for '65 delivers livelier performance *plus* up to 15% better gas economy (a new 170 cu. in. standard Six with optional 3-speed Cruise-O-Matic transmission is the magic formula). Other Falcon economies: a 6-month (or 6000-mile) service schedule. New battery-saving alternator. And, a low, *low* initial price. Is Falcon the best car for the least money this year (best-looking, too)? You can bank on it!

FORD

For new Falcon owners,
the savings go on and on.

The '65 Falcon delivers up to 15% better fuel economy! Two reasons. Falcon's standard Six is now more efficient than ever. And the optional 3-speed Cruise-O-Matic transmission uses engine power more efficiently, too. Other savings: a new battery-saving alternator. Twice-a-year (or 6,000-mile) service schedule. And, of course, the biggest saving of all— Falcon's famous low-low price!

FORD

1965 Falcon ads changed substantially, and featured believe-able-situation illustrations and no-nonsense description content. Layout of these ads provided the basis of the extensive advertising campaign for the new Mustang which commenced in the Spring of 1965.

Falcon 1966

America's Economy Champ...now on its third million
with a sporty new look for '66!

FORD

Early 1966 ad returned to more traditional concept. However, the "Bird" representation (which was also used on early-'66 Sales Catalogs) was considered by many to be too "sinister" and layout was abandoned.

Commuters: Exciting news about
the White Plains Economy Run!

FALCON
Ford

Later in 1966, cleaner, less artistic ad appeared which attempted to return theme to one of Economy.

Models
(initially)

    Type 58A 4-door Sedan
         64A 2-door Sedan

(from 1/6/60)

    Type 59A 2-door station wagon
         71A 4-door station wagon
         66A Ranchero

Options

    Economy Console Radio
    Fresh-air Heater
    I-Rest Tinted Windshield
    Interior, Exterior Deluxe Trim Package:
        Deluxe Upholstery (gray, blue, green)
        White Steering Wheel and Horn Ring
        Rear Seat Arm Rests and Ash Tray
        Front Door Courtesy Switches for Dome Light
        Cigarette Lighter
        Bright-metal Side Window Trim
        Bright-metal Taillight Rings
    Safety Package "A"
        Instrument Panel Safety Padding
        Cushioned Sun Visors
    Ford Seat Belts
    Bright Wheel Rings
    Bright Full Wheel Covers
    Aquamatic Windshield Washer-Wiper
    Inside Non-Glare Rearview Mirror
    Fender Ornaments
    66-Plate, 55 amp-hr Battery
    Fordomatic Drive
    Whitewell Tires

Two very basic models comprised the entire Falcon line when introduced in October of 1959. They were, however, joined in January by the Station Wagons and the Ranchero. With a heavy promotional budget, elaborate advertising commenced and by year-end almost a half million of the "New-Size" Fords had been produced, a first-year record for any new automobile line up to this time.

As with any new product, especially one as involved as a new car, there were problems. The heater control knobs managed to break off due to an unusual requirement that they be fully extended before turned for temperature; a noisy speedometer required a drive gear replacement; ignition switches would bind up; glove box door screws came loose on some cars; air leaks caused some vent windows to whistle uncomfortably; some engines surged and lost power.

Despite all this, Falcon was a very good and extremely reliable car. Filling the market's need for something new and different, the New-Size Ford was to set a first-year production record that would stand until its derivative, the sporty Mustang, introduced some four and a half years later, would break even that record!

Early advertisement stressed Falcon's economy of operation.

Falcon Design: All-new, welded, integral body and frame, with zinc-coated rocker panels and main underbody members, for durability and quietness with high strength-weight ratio. Completely sealed and insulated. Rear-hinged hood with outside safety-type latch. Chromed one-piece front and rear bumpers. Corrosion-resistant aluminum grille. Bright-metal windshield, rear window and drip moldings. Cowl-top ventilation system. Clear-vision safety glass throughout. Wide Angle windshield with forward-slanting pillars. Large, wide-opening doors. Lifeguard Double-Grip door locks. Posture Control front seat, adjustable to 9 positions. Rear-mounted 14-gal. gas tank with Center-Fill fueling.

Engine: 90-hp Falcon Six—144-cu. in. displ.; 3.50" bore x 2.50" stroke; 8.7 to 1 comp. ratio; regular fuel, low-silhouette unit-design carburetor; manual choke; full-vacuum spark control; integral cylinder head and 6-port intake manifold; precision-molded crankshaft with four precision-type main bearings; rotor-type oil pump; oil capacity, with filter change, 4.5 qt.

Features: For economy and long life, the Falcon Six has Short Stroke, low-friction design; Wedge-Type combustion chambers; Free-Turning overhead intake and exhaust valves; 3-ring aluminum-alloy pistons with full-chromed top ring; Super-Filter air cleaner with reusable element; vacuum-booster type fuel pump for more constant windshield-wiper action; full-pressure lubrication system with Full-Flow disposable-type oil filter; pressurized cooling system with 180° Positive-Action thermostat; 12-volt electrical system; weatherproof ignition; 18-mm. Turbo-Action spark plugs; 54-plate, 40 amp-hr battery; positive engagement starter; 3-point rubber-insulated engine mounting; aluminized muffler. Engine is electronically balanced while operating under its own power for optimum smoothness.

Clutch and Manual Transmission: Single cushion disc, dry-plate clutch for smooth engagement; aluminum housing; permanently lubricated ball-bearing type throw-out bearing; suspended clutch pedal for easy action and no draft hole in toeboard. Face diameter is 8½ in. Total frictional area is 67.66 sq. in. 3-*Speed Transmission* has shot-peened fine-pitch helical gears for high strength and quietness with forged bronze synchronizers for smooth operation. Anti-friction bearings throughout. Standard "H" shift pattern with lever on steering column. Ratios (to 1): 1st 3.29, 2nd 1.75, direct 1.00, reverse 4.46.

Fordomatic Drive (optional): Features simplified design with one clutch assembly, lightweight cast-aluminum construction, minimum servicing (each 24,000 miles). Torque converter in combination with compound planetary gear set. Two forward gear ratios, one reverse (to 1): low 1.75, direct 1.00, reverse 1.50; converter (stall) 2.4. In "D" range gives brisk, smooth starts in low. Effective engine braking in "L" position. Air cooled. Selector lever and quadrant on steering column, sequence P-R-N-D-L.

Rear Axle: Semi-floating type with offset hypoid gears. Overhung drive pinion. Induction-hardened forged shafts with permanently lubricated, double-sealed ball-type wheel bearings. Needle roller bearing universal joints. Axle ratios: 3.10 to 1 (standard)—3.56 to 1 (optional).

Front Suspension: Angle-Poised Ball-Joint type with coil springs pivot-mounted and rubber-insulated at top on upper arms for soft ride. Strut-stabilized lower arms. Built-in anti-dive control. Internally mounted hydraulic double-acting shock absorbers with rebound cut-off. Front end has link-type, rubber-bushed ride stabilizer to control roll on turns. Tapered roller wheel bearings.

Rear Suspension: Longitudinal, semi-elliptic leaf springs of asymmetrical design with rear axle located forward from center of springs for anti-squat control on take-off. Provides soft-action, variable-rate with rubber-bushed supports and compression-type shackles for soft, levelized ride. Full length liners between leaves—no lubrication required. Axle nose bumper. Diagonally mounted hydraulic double-acting shock absorbers.

Steering: Magic-Circle low-friction recirculating-ball type steering gear provides easy handling. Protective rear mounting. Anti-friction bearings throughout. Symmetrical linkage. Over-all steering ratio 27 to 1. Lifeguard 17", black, 3-spoke, deep-center steering wheel. Turning diameter 38 ft.

Brakes: Truck Size double-sealed, self-energizing hydraulic brakes have suspended pedal and dash-mounted master cylinder. Composite drums, 9-in. diameter front and rear, with riveted linings, for long life, cool operation and fade resistance. Lining area is 114.3 sq. in. Offset "T" handle parking brake at left of steering column applies rear brakes.

Tires: 6.00 x 13 4-ply, low-profile, black, tubeless with Tyrex cord on 4" safety-type rims. Pressed steel ventilated disc wheels. Spare wheel and tire in luggage compartment.

Standard Equipment: Gray vinyl and nylon cloth interior. Two sun visors. Two front arm rests. Two parallel-action windshield wipers of the dual-range type. Inside rear-view mirror. Instrument panel with speedometer, odometer, fuel gauge, temperature gauge, oil and generator warning lights, high-beam and turn-signal indicators in cluster; lighted control identifications, ash tray, glove box. Dome light operated by headlight switch. Sealed-beam headlights, parking lights, taillights with stoplights and turn signals, license plate light. Sof-Tred black rubber floor covering.

Dimensions: 109.5" wheelbase. Tread: front 55", rear 54.5". Curb weight (est.): 2366 lb. Tudor, 2395 lb. Fordor.

Ford script is molded into face of the headlamps. This practice is continued through 1965, then replaced with similar stamped legend.

1960 Type 64A 2-door Sedan

1960 Type 58A 4-door Sedan

Mr. George Anderson, San Diego, California

Mr. & Mrs. Al Roe, Oceanside, California

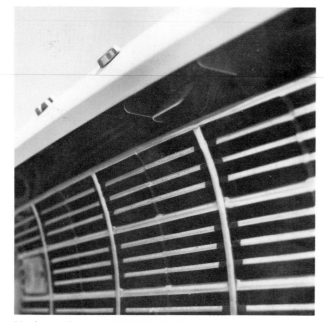

Horizontally-emphasised grill bars are interrupted by spaced vertical lines; grill is recessed behind hood lip.

Distinctive new Falcon grill has headlights, parking/directional lights, and grill completely enclosed by protruding sheet-metal.

Horizontal installation of the parking lights is an identifying feature of the 1960 model.

Parking lights are placed just inboard of headlamps.

Bumper is shaped to provide protective housing for the front license plate.

Adding to appearance, massive bumpers wrap around corners of front fenders.

Forward lip of the hood bears lettered F-O-R-D.

The hood is embossed with a strengthening section which also adds to its appearance.

A chromed Falcon script emblem is affixed to the front fender flanks.

The sculptured fender sections are carried down the sides of the car.

Standard blackwall tires are 6:00 x 13 4-ply, low profile. The 13" wheels have 4" rims.

"FOMOCO" script appears in lower left corner of windshield.

Chromed inside handles are employed on front vent windows.

Windshield corner posts slant straight back; the popular "dogleg" design of the '50's has been eliminated.

The simple wrap-around windshield eliminates complexity and increased cost of compound curves found in earlier full-size cars.

Windshield-wiper arms have stainless steel outer section hinged to chromed inner castings.

A full-width air intake grill is located at the base of the windshield.

Doors are hinged at the front; open from the rear for easy access.

Chromed door handles and outside door locks are standard equipment.

The triangular pane in the rear windows of the 4-door are decorative. Only the forward section lowers to admit air.

The optional Deluxe Trim Package includes polished stainless-steel side window trim (above) which adds to the appearance of the standard painted trim (right).

The rear windows of the 2-door can be lowered for ventilation.

A crisp, thin, roofline and extra-large window area gives the car a well-balanced effect.

The wraparound rear window provides excellent visibility and is trimmed in bright-metal.

The taillights are emphasized by having them recessed behind sculptured surrounding sheet metal. The bright-metal trim ring is a part of the optional Deluxe Trim Package and does not appear on all cars.

A chromed FALCON script emblem appears on the lower right rear panel.

The rear deck lid is hinged to open and offers access to 23 cubic feet of usable storage space.

Easily identifiable Falcon rear end is well styled and emphasizes simplicity of design.

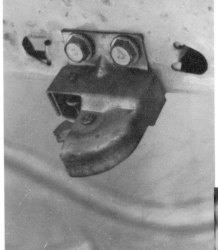

A covered keylock releases the deck latch.

Under the rear deck lid is a latch which locks into a plate affixed to the lower body section (right).

The attractive FORD insignia is actually a useful lift handle. Fuel filler tube is located at lower center and has a plain cap painted to match body.

Luggage compartment floor is protected by a composition floor mat.

The well integrated rear end is emphasized by a full-width massive bumper with protective recess for license plate.

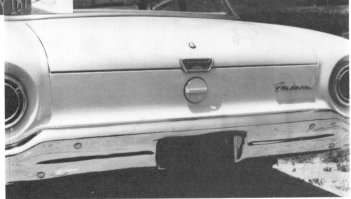

Underside of rear deck lid has X member to strengthen it. Spare wheel is secured in horizontal position.

Hood is held in its closed position by this latch secured to its forward edge.

The Falcon hood is held in its open position by a strut which is hinged at its lower end. Note the strengthening cross member which serves to provide a rigid section.

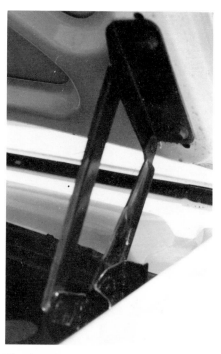

The hood hinges are ingenious assemblies designed to raise hood smoothly.

Still visible is original decal instructing the use of holding bracket for mid-section of hood strut.

The free end of the hood strut is latched under a second bracket to hold safely when hood is closed.

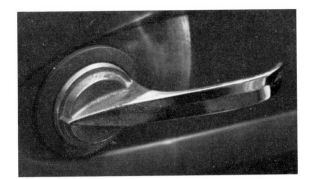

Chromed inside door handles have distinctive appearance.

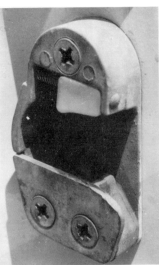

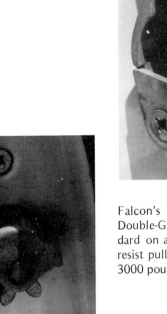

Falcon's Lifeguard Design Double-Grip Door Locks, standard on all models, are said to resist pull-apart forces of up to 3000 pounds!

The standard interior door panels have vertical gray vinyl bars in insert as seen here behind window riser crank arm.

Rugged-appearing doors are well weather-stripped to eliminate drafty interiors.

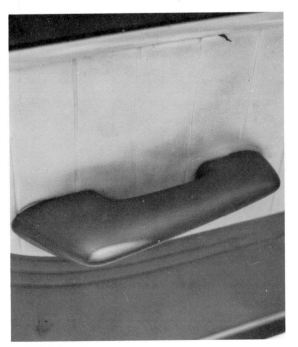

Standard front door arm rests (provided in rear seats only with optional Deluxe Trim Package) are installed with wider section facing rearward.

A Data Plate is affixed to the trailing edge of the left front door. Bearing much information of interest, readers are directed to page 316.

Rear section of inside door sill is enlarged to provide space for an inside locking mechanism. Plastic knob harmonizes with interior colors.

The optional Deluxe Trim Package door panels have blue tweed nylon inserts. (compare previous page)

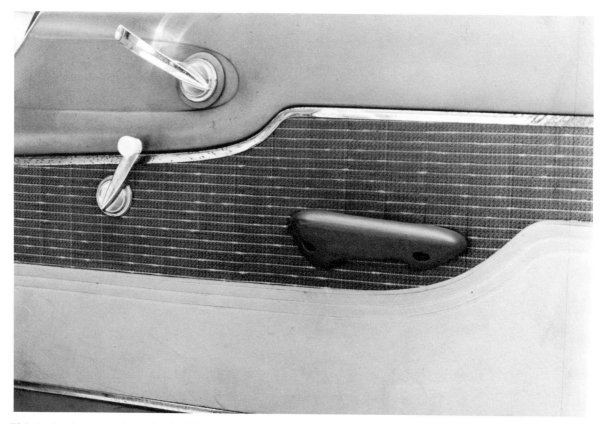

This is the door panel provided with the optional deluxe interior. In general, this replaces the standard gray vinyl bolster and random knitted inserts with the more attractive blue tweed nylon with blue vinyl bolsters.

A well designed instrument panel extends across car with an interesting center dip. The lip of the all-steel panel is optionally covered with protective foamed covering in Safety Package A along with cushioned sun visors.

A push-button latch releases lid of concealed glove box.

Controls for Lights and Wipers are located below left side of the instrument cluster and are identified by legends theron (page 43). Rotating the Light switch knob controls the interior dome light.

Choke and Defrost controls are also identified by legend on instrument cluster (page 43), but heater temperature control bezel is lettered for function.

The standard steering wheel is black, three-spoke, and has a bright-metal horn ring at the hub. Its deep-dish design is a part of Ford's ongoing Lifeguard Design program.

Stylish white plastic knobs are used on both the turn signal control arm and also on the shift lever.

The optional steering wheel, a part of the Deluxe Trim Package, is white, three-spoke, also deep-dished center, and it is provided with a bright-metal horn ring.

The hub of both steering wheels is lettered to display both F-O-R-D and also Falcon.

Falcon's new integrated instrument panel cluster is lighted from behind for nighttime operation. Easily seen through the steering wheel spokes, it presents extremely visible information.

The optional two-speed Fordomatic automatic transmission is provided with a non-illuminated indicator quadrant mounted near steering wheel hub.

Fuel level in rear-mounted tank is indicated by gauge at left side of Instrument Cluster. Rectangular window to its right is illuminated for (low) OIL pressure.

Engine coolant temperature is indicated by matching gauge on right side of Cluster. Rectangular window to its left illuminates GEN to indicate problem in charging circuit.

In keeping with the "economy" slant of Falcon's marketing plan, the only optional radio offered is a manually-tuned version.

Radio control knobs match those of the other controls.

Cigarette lighter is not standard; a blanking plate is. A lighter is an extra cost accessory included in the Deluxe Trim Package.

Engine starter control is on panel-mounted ignition switch which also has an ACCessory position.

The auxiliary rear brakes are applied by pulling lettered handle mounted below left side of instrument panel.

Latching doors are provided on both sides behind and below the Instrument Panel. Opening these doors allows cowl-entry incoming air to flow through the car.

Newly-styled dome lamp is placed at front top center of car just behind sun visors. It's brightly chromed plastic frame holds a transluscent plastic lens.

The standard rear view mirror is shown; an optional non-glare mirror is also available.

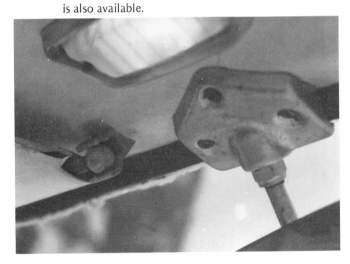

Plastic knobs are furnished at the ends of the sun visors. These snap into plastic clips on the header, or can be released (right) to swing visor to side of car.

The inside rear view mirror shaft is threaded and locked into a three-screw mounting base.

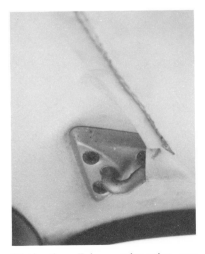

Distinctive Falcon triangular sun visor brackets are finished in flat grey paint; not chromed.

SPECIAL REPORT:

The New Ford Falcon Wagons

ALL THE FACTS AND FIGURES ON THESE TWO NEW-SIZE WAGONS

COMPLETE PRICES ON MODELS, OPTIONS AND ACCESSORIES

EXTRA FEATURE:
First owner reports on the
new 1960 Station Wagons

Falcon's new station wagon was announced on January 6, 1960. Described as having the "longest cargo space and greatest floor load area in its class", it boasted a single-unit welded construction for rigidity and strength and had ample room for six full-sized passengers.

Available in both two-door and four-door models, the cars while appearing larger, were only about 8 inches longer than the sedans although their wheelbase (109½") were the same. In this package was a cargo volume of more than 76 cubic feet, nearly the same as the earlier, and larger, 1957 Ford station wagon! Its maximum cargo floor length of almost nine feet (tailgate extended), is longer, and lower, than any other wagon in the economy car class.

Station Wagon shares same front end treatment as Sedans for easy identification.

1960 Type 71A 4-door Station Wagon

A distinctive sculptured side panel runs the full length of the side of the Station Wagons.

Mr. & Mrs. Dick Griffith, Oceanside, California

The second seat can be folded flat. This latch on right rear wheel housing releases seat back; seat cushion is rotated foward to provide flat cargo floor.

The spare tire is stored vertically in a floor pan depression behind the right rear wheel housing. A plastic cover (not shown) protects the exposed half. Cargo floor mat is ribbed rubber mat; carpeting seen here is Owner's installation.

Only the rectangular section of the 4-door rear door glass can be lowered; other portion is fixed. 2-door models omit this feature.

Two-door wagons omit the rear door seen here. By eliminating the necessary dogleg over the wheel housing required for this rear door, the two-door wagon can accept a full-width rear window (page 140).

Rear window is equipped with a standard manual crank. An optional electric, key-operated, rear window control is also available.

Station Wagon's counter-balanced tailgate features a roll-down window. The rear opening is 45½ inches wide by 27" high.

The tailgate ornament, while similar to that on sedan rear deck, (page 37) differs in that it lies flat against body, does not serve as lift handle.

The tailgate is latched in its closed position by this lever-operated mechanism. Its hard rubber knob can be depressed into a rectangular slot to prohibit release of the tailgate latch.

FORD *Falcon* '61

THE WORLD'S MOST SUCCESSFUL NEW CAR

New Measure of Compact Car Value

Type 58A 4-door Sedan
64A 2-door Sedan
59A 2-door Station Wagon
71A 4-door Station Wagon
66A Ranchero
78A Sedan Delivery
89C Station Bus
89B Club Wagon
89D Deluxe Club Wagon

Options & Accessories
Radio; manual or push-button tuned
Fresh Air Heater
Fordomatic
Deluxe Trim and/or Ornamentation Packages
170 Special Six Engine
PolarAire Conditioner
Anti-Fume Crankcase Ventilation System
Two Tone Paint Combinations
Luggage Rack (wagons)
Electric Windshield Wipers
Windshield Washer
I-Rest Tinted Windshield
Fender Ornaments
Full Wheel Covers
Wheel Trim Rings
Whitewall Tires
Locking Gas Cap
License Plate Frames
Full-View Mirrors
Inside Non-Glare Mirror
Spotlight
Seat Covers
Ventilated Seat Cushions

New for 1961, the Sedan Delivery was a stylish commercial vehicle.

1961 brought new models to the Falcon line. An attractive Sedan Delivery was introduced and Van-styled Station Bus and Club Wagon models also appeared. The Sedan Delivery resembled the 2-door Station Wagon with the mid-and the rear-quarter windows closed in. The vans, however, were built on the basic now-familar "Econoline" concept and later were to be considered as only a part of that line despite their clear Falcon parentage.

The Falcon continued to be heavily promoted as an "Economy Car", and when they won both First and Second place in the 1961 Mobilgas Economy Run from Los Angeles to Chicago, the triumph was heavily promoted. Noting that the winning fuel economy was 32.6 miles-per-gallon, it is interesting to compare with contemporary achievements.

New options for 1961 included, in addition to Two-Tone paint combinations, such items as PolarAire Conditioning, a new 101 horsepower Special Six engine, and push-button radio.

SPECIFICATIONS

FALCON DESIGN: Welded, integral body and frame for quietness and high strength-weight ratio. Completely sealed and insulated. Roof cross brace at center on sedans and three roof cross braces on wagons give extra rigidity. Zinc-coated rocker panels and main underbody members for durability. Thicker anodized, corrosion-resistant aluminum grille. Large, wide-opening doors, with assist-type door checks. Lifeguard Double-Grip door locks. Wagons have easy-to-operate counterbalanced tailgate (with coil assist springs), roll-down tailgate window and Stowaway 2nd seat. Choice of Single Colors—11 on sedans, 12 on wagons—in gleaming, durable Diamond Lustre Finish.

ENGINES: 85-hp Falcon Six—144-cu. in. displ.; 3.50" bore x 2.50" stroke; 8.7 to 1 comp. ratio; regular fuel; low-silhouette unit-design carburetor; manual choke; oil capacity, with filter change, 4.5 qt.

101-hp Falcon 170 Special Six—170-cu. in. displ.; 3.50" bore x 2.94" stroke; 8.7 to 1 comp. ratio; regular fuel; low-silhouette unit-design carburetor; manual choke; oil capacity, with filter change, 4.5 qt.

ENGINE FEATURES: For economy and long life, Falcon engines have short-stroke, low-friction design; Free-Turning overhead intake and exhaust valves; integral cylinder head and 6-port intake manifold; Super-Filter air cleaner; vacuum-booster type fuel pump; Full-Flow oil filter; 12-volt electrical system; 18-mm. Turbo-Action spark plugs; aluminized muffler. Engines are electronically balanced while operating under their own power for optimum smoothness.

CLUTCH AND MANUAL TRANSMISSION: Single cushion disc, dry-plate clutch; aluminum housing; suspended clutch pedal. 3-Speed Transmission has helical gears with forged bronze synchronizers for smooth operation. Gear ratios tailored to each engine. Lever on steering column.

FORDOMATIC DRIVE (optional): A 2-speed automatic featuring simplified design, lightweight cast-aluminum construction, minimum servicing. In "D" range gives brisk, smooth starts in low. Effective engine braking in "L" position. Selector lever and quadrant on steering column.

REAR AXLE: Semi-floating type with offset hypoid gears. Induction-hardened forged shafts with permanently lubricated wheel bearings.

FRONT SUSPENSION: Angle-Poised Ball-Joint type with pivoted, top-mounted coil springs. Strut-stabilized lower arms. New threaded, permanently lubricated bushings in upper arms and rubber bushings in lower arms for softer ride. Built-in anti-dive control. Double-acting shock absorbers. Link-type, rubber-bushed ride stabilizer.

REAR SUSPENSION: Semi-elliptic leaf springs with reduced spring rate, rubber-bushed supports and compression-type shackles, giving variable-rate characteristics for a softer, more levelized ride. Asymmetrical design for anti-squat on take-off. Full length liners between leaves. Double-acting shock absorbers.

STEERING: Magic-Circle recirculating-ball type. Anti-friction bearings throughout. Over-all ratio 27 to 1. Lifeguard 17", black, 3-spoke, deep-center steering wheel. Turning diameter approx. 38 ft.

BRAKES: Double-sealed, self-energizing hydraulic, 9-in. diameter front and rear. Total lining area 131.0 sq. in. on sedans, 150.6 sq. in. on wagons. Suspended pedal, dash-mounted master cylinder.

TIRES: Soft-Tread design, black, tubeless with Tyrex cord. Safety-type rims. Sedans—6.00 x 13 4-ply on 4" rims; Wagons—6.50 x 13 4-ply on 4½" rims.

DIMENSIONS: 109.5" wheelbase. Tread: front 55", rear 54.5". Height: sedans 54.5", wagons 55.1". Width 70.6". Over-all length: sedans 181.2", wagons 189".

STANDARD EQUIPMENT: Two sun visors and front arm rests. Parallel action, vacuum-boosted windshield wipers. Instrument panel with lighted control identifications, ash tray, glove box. Dome light operated by headlight switch. Foam-padded front seat (also rear seat in wagons). Coat hooks. Dual horns.

A deluxe trim option provided the 1961 Falcon sedans with a bright-metal strip which highlighted the sculptured sides.

1961 Type 58A 4-Door Sedan

Dr. Stuart Nordstrom, Oceanside, California

1961 Parking Lamps are installed in a vertical position, a clear identification feature.

1961 grill is convex as opposed to the 1960 grill which is concave (page 32).

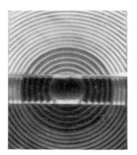

Similar in appearance to the 1960 style, the parking light lens is actually quite different.

Convex grill and vertical parking lights quickly identify the 1961 model.

The hood is unchanged from the 1961 model.

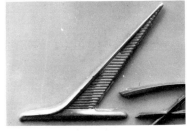

A stylized Falcon emblem is added to the chromed script on the front fender flanks.

Sculptured side indents are unchanged from 1960.

Replacements for Falcon's bolt-on front fenders, were offered at only $25.95 each at the time!

In addition to the standard 9" wheelcover, Ford offered an optional Deluxe Wheelcover (page 294).

Optional Deluxe Body Side Trim adds bright metal trim to highlight edges of indents.

Bright-metal windshield molding and rain gutters are standard.

Side window frames are painted, but a Deluxe Trim Package provides bright-metal trim at this point.

The door handles and locks are unchanged.

Doors of the Sedans are hinged at the front to allow easy access.

View is unchanged from 1960 (page 34); new insignia on front fender (previous page) would be marked difference.

Full-width rear window is framed in attractive bright-metal trim. Although a tinted windshield was availabe in 1961, no offering was made of tinted side- or rear-windows.

The rear deck lid lock is unchanged.

Lettered F-A-L-C-O-N now appears at the rear replacing script nameplate used in 1960 (page 36). Fuel cap seen here is an aftermarket accessory.

The Ford Crest emblem is again used as a lift handle in 1961.

Deluxe exterior bright-metal side trim extends around the rear tail light housing.

The Deluxe Exterior Trim Package includes these polished aluminum taillight trim rings which are installed over the standard lenses.

Standard taillight lens assumes different appearance without the dress-up trim.

F-A-L-C-O-N lettering at the rear is distinctive 1961 identification. Fuel cap is aftermarket accessory.

Inside door handle with its plastic spacer continues unchanged.

Front door arm rests are now installed with wider section forward (compare page 39).

Inside window crank is unchanged.

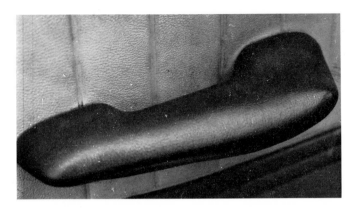

Data Plate on rear edge of left front door is continued.

Standard interior door panel is shown. An optional Deluxe Interior is offered with tweed nylon inserts and vinyl bolsters. Color choice of this optional interior has been expanded to four; blue, green, gray, or turquoise.

An unchanged horn button is placed at the hub of the steering wheel.

The standard three-speed transmission is shifted by a column-mounted lever equipped with a white plastic knob.

Turn signal lever, mounted at left just below steering wheel, has a matching white plastic knob.

An accessory aftermarket steering wheel wrap has been installed for the owner's comfort.

A redesigned mirror mount now supports visor ends on which the knobs have been eliminated (page 45).

Unchanged threaded mirror shaft is threaded and locked into the revised mount.

The appearance of the 1961 Instrument Cluster is familiar since it is unchanged from that used in the 1960 Falcon.

Parking brake handle remains under the left side of instrument panel.

Heater controls are as used in 1960; blanking plate covers access hole for optional cigarette lighter.

Two optional radios are offered for 1961. One is push-button tuned (top photo), the other is the "economy radio", a manual-tuned version.

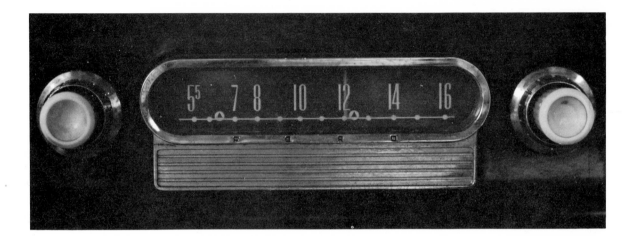

The Fresh Air Heater is an optional installation and blanking plates are provided to cover pre-punched control knob shaft holes when heater is not ordered.

There is no change in the ignition lock or its placement on the lower left of the instrument panel.

Layout of the back-lighted Instrument Cluster is unchanged. OIL and GEN warning lights are continued as shown.

The 100 mph speedometer has large and easily readable reference scale numbers.

1961 Type 66A Ranchero

The 1961 Ford Falcon Ranchero continued to offer style and economy. Its full-size passenger compartment had ample room for three adults and its big six foot box offered almost 32 cu. ft. of cargo area. Tests with the standard 85 horsepower SIX resulted in fuel economy of 38.3 miles per gallon!

An optional Deluxe Trim Package includes bright-metal molding around the box and cab back; bright-metal taillight trim rings; bright-metal door window moldings; white steering wheel with horn ring; cigarette lighter; dome light door switch; plus the black-and-white or red-and-white vinyl upholstery.

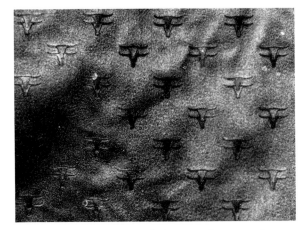

The standard interior of the Ranchero employs a unique brown "Western Motif" insert with beige vinyl bolsters.

Mr. Harry Meverden, Oceanside, California

Chromed Ranchero script is placed on fender flanks.

Forward portion of vehicle has unmistaken appearance of the 1961 Falcon.

FOMOCO script and additional information as to date of manufacture is found in the original window glass.

Door handles and locks (right) are identical to those used on Sedans.

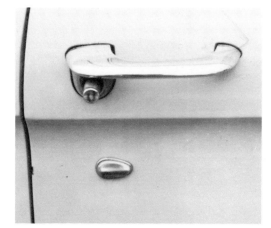

Although the rear portion of vehicle differs greatly, Ranchero fenders and doors interchange with those of 2-door Sedans and Wagons.

Door frames of Ranchero are painted. The Deluxe Trim Option provides add-on bright-metal trim.

Standard taillight lens is untrimmed.

Standard trim at the back of cab and around box is painted.

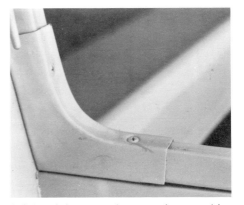

A formed sheet metal corner piece provides smooth transition behind cab.

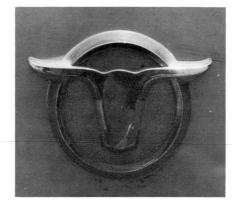

A distinctive emblem appears on the tailgate. Although a nice styling feature, its principal purpose is to conceal opening for the Station Wagon's rear window crank as this is the same tailgate used thereon.

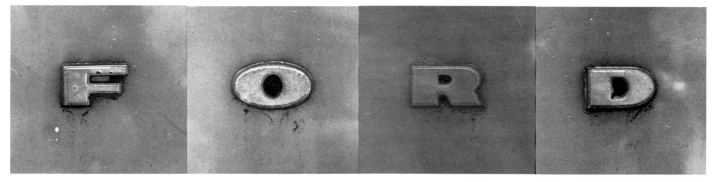

These letters appear on the hood lip of all 1960/61 models and on the tailgate of the Ranchero.

The counterbalanced tailgate is easy to load. When lowered, it is only about 27" from the ground and has a clear opening of over 40". Closed, its top is about 38.9" from the ground. It is latched with the same mechanism as the Wagon (page 49).

Early Sales Folder, printed in August of 1961, featured 4-door Sedan with optional deluxe trim on cover.

Models

Type 58A 4-door Sedan
59A 2-door Station Wagon
64A 2-door Sedan
64C Futura 2-door Sedan with Bucket Seats
66A Ranchero
71A 4-door Station Wagon
71B Squire Wagon
78A Sedan Delivery
89C Station Bus
89B Club Wagon
89D Deluxe Club Wagon
(mid-year)
62C Sports Futura

Mid-Year Sales Folder, (March 1962), displayed new Sports Futura with optional vinyl-covered roof.

Initially, 1962 models included the new Futura 2-door, the 2- and 4-door wagons and sedans, the Ranchero, Sedan Delivery, the Falcon Squire, and the new Station Bus, Club Wagon, and Deluxe Club Wagon, these three being "van" type vehicles built on a 90" wheelbase, with Falcon's six-cylinder engines, and employing some Falcon trim items.

The new Futura had a standard bucket seat interior complete with Thunderbird-like console and a special Futura side trim. The Falcon Squire was a deluxe 4-door wagon with simulated wood grain sides, standard power tailgate, carpeting, and bright-metal window trim. An optional top Luggage Rack added much to its appearance.

In mid-year, a new model, the Sports Futura, made its appearance. Featuring a new roofline, the car also was the first in the line to offer the popular optional 4-speed manual transmission which was then made available for other models.

Options and Accessories
Lifeguard Jr. Rear Door Locks
Padded Dash & white Padded Visors
Seat Belts
2-speed Electric Wipers
Windshield Washer
PolarAire Conditioner
Falcon Fordomatic
Fresh Air Heater
Push Button Radio
 (Manual radio on Station Bus & Club Wagons)
Wagon Top Luggage Rack
170 Special Six Engine
17 Two Tone Paint Combinations
54 Plate-55 Amp-Hr Battery

Rayon Cord Tires
Wheel Trim Rings
License Plate Frames
Back Up Lights
Power Tailgate Window
Deluxe Solid Wheelcovers
Spotlight
Locking Gas Cap
Outside mirrors and inside Non-Glare Mirror
I-Rest Tinted Glass
Seat Covers
 mid year:
Vinyl Roof for Sports Futura
4-speed Transmission

SPECIFICATIONS

The Ford Quality Control system, a Ford first, results in products of highest quality. All manufactured parts pass rigid dimensional, laboratory and durability tests. Quality Control teams also select cars from each shift at every assembly plant for an exhaustive search for any deviations from strict engineering specifications.

FALCON DESIGN: Welded, integral body and frame for quietness and high strength-weight ratio. Completely sealed and insulated. Roof cross braces at center on sedans and three roof cross braces on wagons give extra rigidity. Zinc-coated rocker panels and main underbody members for durability. Cowl-top ventilation. Wide Angle windshield with forward-slanting pillars. Large, wide-opening doors, with assist-type door checks and bronze-bushed hinges. Double-Grip door locks. Rear-mounted 14-gal. gas tank with Center-Fill fueling on sedans, left rear fender fuel fill on wagons, Station Bus and Club Wagons.

ENGINES: 85-hp Falcon Six—144-cu. in. displ.; 3.50" bore x 2.50" stroke; 8.7 to 1 comp. ratio; regular fuel; new low-silhouette unit-design carburetor; manual choke; oil capacity, with filter change, 4.5 qt.
101-hp Falcon 170 Special Six—170-cu. in. displ.; 3.50" bore x 2.94" stroke; 8.7 to 1 comp. ratio; regular fuel; new low-silhouette unit-design carburetor; manual choke; oil capacity, with filter change, 4.5 qt.

FEATURES: For greater economy and longer life, Falcon engines have short-stroke, low-friction design; Wedge-Type combustion chambers; Free-Turning overhead intake and exhaust valves; 3-ring aluminum-alloy pistons with full-chromed top ring; integral cylinder head and 6-port intake manifold; precision-molded crankshaft with four main bearings; rotor-type pump; Super-Filter dry-type air cleaner with reusable element (oil-bath air cleaner in Station Bus, Club Wagons); 6,000-mile high-capacity in-line fuel filter (4,000-mile filter in Station Bus, Club Wagons); vacuum-booster type fuel pump for more constant windshield wiper action; full-pressure lubrication system with Full-Flow disposable-type oil filter; pressurized cooling system with 190° Positive-Action thermostat; 2-yr. or 30,000-mile engine coolant-antifreeze (available—installed in production); 12-volt electrical system; weatherproof ignition; 18-mm. Turbo-Action spark plugs; 54-plate, 40 amp-hr battery; positive engagement starter; fully aluminized muffler. Engines electronically mass-balanced while operating under their own power for optimum smoothness.

CLUTCH AND MANUAL TRANSMISSIONS: Single cushion disc, dry-plate clutch for smooth engagement; aluminum housing; permanently lubricated ball-bearing type throw-out bearing. Face diameter is 8½". Total frictional area is 68.1 sq. in. **3-Speed Transmission** (std.) fine-pitch helical gears treated for high strength and quietness with forged bronze synchronizers in 2nd and direct for smooth operation. Anti-friction bearings throughout. Standard "H" shift pattern with lever on steering column. Ratios (to 1): 1st 3.29, 2nd 1.75 (1.83 with 170 Special Six), direct 1.00, reverse 4.46; (Station Bus, Club Wagons: 1st 3.39, 2nd 1.97, direct 1.00, reverse 4.12). **4-Speed Transmission** (opt.) has floor-mounted "short stick" shift lever, with shift pattern on knob. All forward gears synchronized for fast, smooth shifting. Available with any Falcon model and engine except Station Bus, Club Wagons. Ratios (to 1): 1st 3.16, 2nd 2.21, 3rd 1.41, direct 1.00, reverse 3.35.

FORDOMATIC DRIVE (optional with any Falcon model and engine except Station Bus, Club Wagons): Features simplified design, lightweight cast-aluminum construction, new vacuum-controlled throttle valve for smoothness, minimum servicing. Torque converter

in combination with compound planetary gear set. Gear ratios (to 1): low 1.75, direct 1.00, reverse 1.50; converter (stall) 2.4. In "D" range gives brisk, smooth starts in low. Effective engine braking in "L" position. Air-cooled with 144 Six, air- and liquid-cooled with 170 Special Six. Selector lever and quadrant on steering column, sequence P-R-N-D-L.

REAR AXLE: Semi-floating type with offset hypoid gears. Induction-hardened forged shafts with permanently lubricated wheel bearings. **Axle Ratios** (to 1): **3-Speed Manual**—Sedans: 3.10 with std. Six, 3.20 with Special Six (3.50 opt., either engine)—All Wagons and Bus: 3.50 with both engines; 4.00 opt. with std. Six only. **4-Speed Manual**—Sedans: 3.10 with std. Six (3.50 opt.); 3.50 with Special Six (3.20 opt.)—Wagons: 3.50 with both engines; 4.00 opt. with std. Six only. **Fordomatic Drive**—Sedans and wagons: 3.50 with both engines; 4.00 opt. with std. Six on wagons.

FRONT SUSPENSION: Sedans and wagons—Angle-Poised Ball-Joint type with coil springs pivot-mounted on upper arms. Strut-stabilized lower arms. Threaded, permanently lubricated bushings in upper arms and rubber bushings in lower arms for softer ride. Built-in anti-dive control. Internally mounted hydraulic double-acting shock absorbers with rebound cutoff. Link-type, rubber-bushed ride stabilizer. Tapered roller wheel bearings. (Station Bus and Club Wagons have solid front axle and leaf springs.)

REAR SUSPENSION: Sedans and wagons—Longitudinal, semi-elliptic leaf springs with rubber-bushed supports and compression-type shackles, giving variable-rate characteristics for a softer, more levelized ride. Asymmetrical design with rear axle located forward from center of springs for anti-squat control on take-off. Full-length liners between leaves—no lubrication required. Diagonally mounted hydraulic double-acting shock absorbers. (Station Bus and Club Wagons have front and rear leaf springs similar to the type described.)

STEERING: Magic-Circle low-friction recirculating-ball type steering gear provides easy handling. Anti-friction bearings throughout. Over-all steering ratio—sedans and wagons: 27 to 1; Station Bus and Club Wagons: 20 to 1. Turning diameter—sedans and wagons: 38.8 ft.; Station Bus and Club Wagons: 34.8 ft.

BRAKES: Double-sealed, self-energizing hydraulic with composite drums. Diameter, front and rear: 9 in. on sedans and wagons, 10 in. on Station Bus and Club Wagons. Molded linings for long life and fade resistance. Total lining area 131.0 sq. in. on sedans, 157 sq. in. on wagons; 168 sq. in. on Station Bus and Club Wagons.

TIRES: Soft-Tread design, black, tubeless with Tyrex Rayon cord, safety-type rims. Sedans—6.00 x 13 on 4" rims; All Wagons—6.50 x 13 on 4½" rims; (optional 7.00 x 13 6-ply required with 2nd, or 2nd and 3rd seat options in Station Bus, Club Wagons). Spare wheel and tire location: Sedans—luggage compartment; Wagons, Station Bus and Club Wagons—cargo area behind right-hand wheelhousing.

CURB WEIGHTS (approx.): Sedans—2370 lb. Tudor, 2410 lb. Fordor, 2450 lb. Sports Futura; Wagons—2670 lb. Tudor, 2700 lb. Fordor, 2740 lb. Falcon Squire. Station Bus 2800 lb., Deluxe Club Wagon 3060 lb. For dimensions see illustrations at right.

1962 Type 64A 2-door Sedan with Deluxe Trim Option

Sloping rear window pillar identifies the earlier (and continuing) Two-Door Sedan.

Mr. & Mrs. Jim McIlrath, Oceanside, California

These letters appear on the hood lip of all 1962/63 Falcons and on the tailgate of the Ranchero. These same letters are later to be found on the tailgate of the 1964/65 Ranchero as well.

Headlights are recessed behind bright-metal bezel.

Hood release latch handle protrudes through lower grill center.

Parking lights now appear in the bumper. Lens is frosted white.

New grill is moved out at the top and now meets the forward lip of the hood.

A new hood for 1962 has a wider wind split than previously, and is provided with a chromed "intake" trim.

A Sedan Deluxe Trim Option includes Bright Metal Window Frames; Rear Quarter Trim and Side Moldings; Fender Top Ornaments; Choice of seven pleated Nylon and Vinyl or all-vinyl interior trims; wall-to-wall carpets; arm rests and ash trays, front and rear; Cigarette Lighter; Deluxe White Steering Wheel with Chrome Horn Ring; Dome Light operated by Front Door Courtesy Switches.

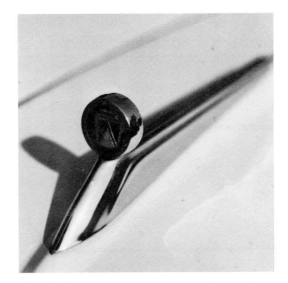

The fender top ornaments are part of the Deluxe Trim Option.

Gold-anodized fender side trim resembles 1961 style (page 55), but differs by the increased length of its horizontal arm. Falcon script is unchanged.

Chromed trim at lower sculpture edge is part of the Deluxe Trim Option.

The shape of front fender sculptured indent has been revised (page 55).

Falcon's parallel-acting standard dual windshield wipers continue.

Standard vent windows are latched with a chromed knob.

Pushbutton door handles and keylock cover are chromed as in the past.

Bright-Metal side moldings are part of Deluxe Trim Option offered for the Sedans.

Optional Deluxe Side Trim has unique cross section.

Deluxe Side Trim also includes a bright-metal panel at rear fender lower quarter.

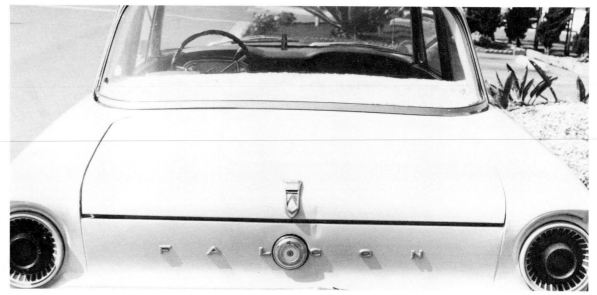

Letters F-A-L-C-O-N appear on rear of 1962 Sedans. A new Ornament now conceals the rear deck lid keylock.

An optional gas cap was offered in 1962. This one is aftermarket; correct cap appears on page 302.

Sculptured fender surrounds the taillight assembly and emphasizes its appearance.

Distinctive taillight bezels are an identifying feature for 1962.

The optional Deluxe Trim Package includes these rear seat arm rests with integral ash trays.

This Ford script emblem appears on the door panel of the right door only, in the 1962 Falcons.

Front door sill scuff plates are formed aluminum.

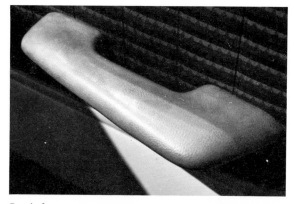

Dual front arm rests, shown here on Deluxe Trim panel, are standard in all models.

Vehicle's data plate is found on rear edge of left front door.

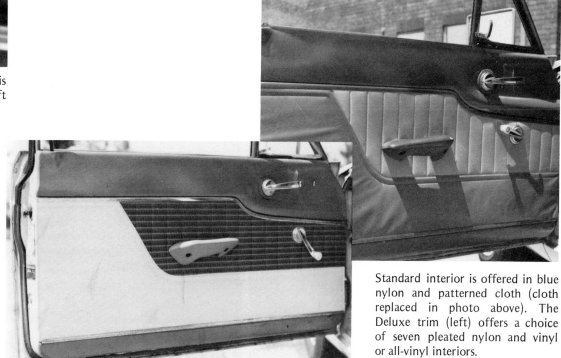

Standard interior is offered in blue nylon and patterned cloth (cloth replaced in photo above). The Deluxe trim (left) offers a choice of seven pleated nylon and vinyl or all-vinyl interiors.

Standard steering wheel is unchanged, again a three-spoke, deep dish, provided with a bright-metal horn button at its hub.

Again the optional Deluxe Trim Package provides a three-spoke white steering wheel with horn ring. Both wheels and caps are unchanged from 1960. Steering wheel rim leather wrap seen here is owner-added.

The deluxe horn "ring" is actually an incomplete ring. One segment is omitted for better visibility.

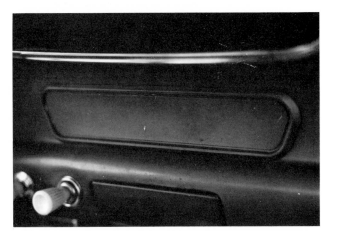

Radio options again include a push-button model for sedans and wagons; a manual-tuned in Club Wagon and Station Bus.

When not optioned, a blanking plate is provided to cover a pierced radio mounting hole in the instrument panel.

Optional foam-padded instrument panel cover is trimmed with bright-metal on its lower edge only.

Transmission shift lever is furnished with a white knob.

A new black instrument cluster dial changes the appearance of the panel.

The fuel gauge assembly is identical from 1960-62.

Likewise, the temperature gauge is the same from 1960-62.

Illuminated GEN light is displayed when charging circuit is inoperative.

Standard white knobs continue to be used on other then the Futura model. Futura knobs (page 89) have chromed center.

Early 1962 hood continues to be held open with a hinged strut. On cars built after December 1, 1962, a new spring-loaded counterbalanced hood hinge was used and the strut omitted (photo lower right).

Both the 85 horsepower 144 cubic inch SIX and the 101 hp 170 cubic inch Special SIX were offered again in 1962.

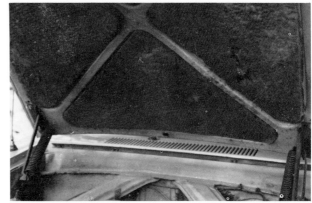

Initially, a new "Futura" two-door sedan appeared. This was a dressed-up version of the standard 2-door Sedan whose most interesting feature was its standard front bucket seats and console. Despite the same bright metal trim listed below, (except for the roof quarter ornament, this model, the 64C, was attractive, but not especially notable.

Replacing it as a mid-year model, the Sports Futura was Falcon's "Lively One". With a new Thunderbird-like roofline and dressed-up interiors, the car offered a new and exciting Option, the manual 4-speed transmission with a floor-mounted stick shift.

Standard equipment included front bucket seats and center console; a choice of five all-vinyl interior trims; white whipcord head-lining; special Futura arm rests and ash trays front and rear; Bright-metal trim which included: Emblem on glove compartment door, front fender side ornament, side spear, rear quarter "Futura" script, Futura block letters on rear panel, and a "gold" Falcon emblem on roof rear quarter; also Sports Futura Full Wheel Covers.

A new Luxury Roof Option provided a padded and trimmed vinyl roof covering in black or white leather-look vinyl for even greater elegance.

So special was the Sports Futura that the Falcon catalog was moved to call it the "compact cousin of the Thunderbird".

1962 Type 62C Sports Futura

"Formal" look of the rear roofline was the distinctive styling change introduced by the Sports Futura.

Mr. Doug Nickerson, Fallbrook, California

New front fender ornament and side spear are unique to the Sports Futura model although both were initially used on the earlier Futura two-door.

Front fender ornament presents distinctive arrow-like appearance.

Bright-metal side window trim is standard on the Sports Futura.

Side spears run from front fender down length of car to the back of the rear fender.

Rear roof quarter emblem is distinctive new golden Futura ornament.

New body trim includes this piece at the base of rear roof pillar.

Futura chromed script appears on rear fenders.

F-U-T-U-R-A appears in block letters at the rear replacing the F-A-L-C-O-N used on the sedans. Note aftermarket locking gas cap.

Sports Futura includes the white three-spoke steering wheel and chromed horn ring.

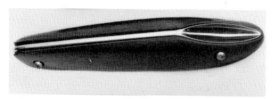

These front arm rests are unique to the 1962 Futura.

Typical of the special dress-up items are these chromed hinge covers for Futura's bucket seats.

Door panel is the Deluxe Interior panel for 1962 which, with bucket seats, is the standard Futura interior.

New for 1962 are these white knobs with chromed centers. They are introduced on the Futura and are to be continued for the following model year.

1962 FORD TRUCKS
FALCON—RANCHERO PICKUP AND SEDAN DELIVERY

Side view mirrors are after-market accessories.

1962 Sales Folder combined Ranchero and Sedan Delivery in one publication.

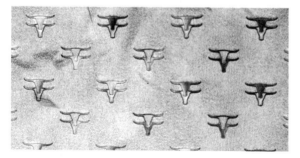

Standard interior was again this "Western Motif" vinyl with beige bolsters. A Deluxe Trim Package included Black-and-White or Red-and-White vinyl interiors.

1962 Type 66A Ranchero

In tests conducted on hills, level ground, and simulated traffic conditions, Falcon's 85 horsepower SIX averaged well over 30 miles per gallon. This fuel economy was widely advertised in the promotion of the Ranchero and Sedan Delivery. At the time fuel costs were not an especially big factor in commercial vehicle costs, but in light of contemporary conditions, it would appear that Ford was on the right track.

Trim was sparce, but an optional Deluxe Trim Package included bright-metal moldings on door window frames and the tailgate window opening plus arm rests on both front doors, and right-hand sun visor on Sedan Delivery Ranchero Deluxe Trim Package included bright-metal moldings around top of box and cab back plus window frames. Both included the white steering wheel with horn ring; cigarette lighter; dome light door switch; and black-and-white or red-and-white vinyl upholstery.

Mr. Swede Anderson, San Diego, California

The unchanged Ranchero cargo box provides over 31½ cubic feet of load space. Lifting loads into it is eased by its maximum 38.9" height of the sides above the ground. Lowered tailgate is even less, only 27 inces from the ground.

Distinctive chromed Ranchero script is placed in fender inset.

Many owners added oversize rear view mirrors, especially when towing large loads as smaller size of Ranchero pickup was often dwarfed by trailer loads it could pull.

Bright metal Full Wheel Covers were an available accessory. See page 294 for standard wheelcover.

The trim on the back of the cab and around the box top is painted in standard form. The Deluxe Trim Package, an option, provides bright-metal dress-up.

The flat rear window of the Ranchero is installed with a plain black rubber gasket.

Sculptured side inserts add rigidity to rear quarters.

FALCON for '63

1963 Sales Folder, printed in 8/62 featured the exciting new Convertible.

FALCON for 63!

1963 Sales Folder, printed in December of 1962 showed the new Futura Hardtop with vinyl roof option.

Final 1963 Sales Folder, dated 2/63 introduces the V-8 engine as the latest Falcon Option.

Models

Type 54A 4-door Sedan
54B Futura 4-door Sedan
59A 2-door Station Wagon
59B Deluxe 2-door Station Wagon
62B 2-door Sedan
62B Futura 2-door Sedan
62C 2-door Sedan (Bucket Seats)
63B Futura 2-door Hardtop
63C Futura 2-door Sports Coupe (Bucket Seats)
66A Ranchero
66B Deluxe Ranchero
71A 4-door Station Wagon
71B Futura 4-door Station Wagon
71C 4-door Squire
71D 4-door Super Deluxe Squire
76A Convertible
76B Convertible (Bucket Seats)
78A Sedan Delivery
78B Deluxe Sedan Delivery
89C Station Bus
89B Club Wagon
89D Deluxe Club Wagon

FALCON for 63!
NOW WITH V-8's

For 1963, Falcon seemed to come of age. A new Futura Convertible model was offered, featuring the conventional full-width bench seat, and a Futura Sports Convertible offered Bucket Seats and a center console. A new lineup of Futuras included both 2-and 4-door Sedans and a Sports Sedan, all with the "Thunderbird inspired" rear roof line. New "standard" Falcon Sedans resembled the Futura but lacked their upgraded trim, and five wagons, two Club Wagons, and a Station Bus completed the initial lineup.

In January, a new Futura Hardtop appeared in both a bench seat and a bucket seat model. Featuring a new slant to its windshield and a crisp roof line, it was the basis for the still further upgraded 1963½ Sprint Hardtop (and Sprint Convertible) which were initially offered with six-cylinder engines although few were built that way.

Finally, in February, the availability of a new V-8 engine was announced, the 260 cubic inch 164 horsepower Challenger. This engine, with chromed dress up items including valve covers and air cleaner, became standard in the Sprint Hardtop and Convertible; optional in other models.

OPTIONS AND ACCESSORIES

Push-button All-Transistor Radio
Ford Air Conditioner
Electric Clock
Wheelcovers
Back Up Lights
Padded Instrument Panel & Visors
Seat Belts
Power Steering
Floor Mats
Rear Seat Radio Speaker
Spotlight with Mirror
Several Outside Mirrors

Two-Tone Paint
White Sidewall Tires
2-Speed Electric Wipers
Windshield Washer
Cigarette Lighter
StudioSonic Rear Seat Radio Speaker
Door Edge Moldings
Rocker Panel Moldings
Locking Gas Cap
Wheel Trim Rings
Seat Covers
Etc.

ENGINES: 85-hp Falcon Six (standard all models except Sprints and Futura convertibles)—144 cu. in. displ.; 3.50" bore x 2.50" stroke; 8.7 to 1 comp. ratio; regular fuel; single-barrel carburetor; manual choke; oil capacity, incl. filter, 4.5 qt.; single exhaust system.

101-hp Falcon 170 Special Six (standard on Futura convertibles, optional all other models except Sprints)—170 cu. in. displ.; 3.50" bore x 2.94" stroke. Other specifications same as Falcon Six above.

164-hp Challenger 260 V-8 (optional all models except Sprints)—260 cu. in. displ.; 3.80" bore x 2.87" stroke; 8.7 to 1 comp. ratio; regular fuel; 2-barrel carburetor; automatic choke; oil capacity, incl. filter, 5 qt.; single exhaust system.

164-hp Sprint 260 V-8 (standard on Sprints)—same as Challenger 260 V-8 plus special trim items, power-toned air cleaner and muffler.

ENGINE FEATURES: For inherent economy and longer life, Falcon engines have short-stroke, low-friction design; Wedge-Type combustion chambers; aluminized intake and exhaust valves on V-8's; hydraulic lifters for automatic valve adjustment; integrally cast cylinder head and manifold on Sixes; alternate intake and exhaust ports on V-8's; 3-ring aluminum-alloy pistons with full-chromed top ring; precision-molded crankshaft with 4 main bearings, (5 on V-8's); rotor-type oil pump; Super-Filter 24,000-mile (Six), 30,000-mile (V-8), dry-type air cleaner element; full-pressure lubrication system with Full-Flow disposable-type oil filter; 6,000-mile oil and filter change interval; high-capacity 36,000-mile or 2-yr. engine coolant (available —installed in production); pressurized cooling system with 190° thermostat; 12-volt electrical system; weatherproof ignition with air-cooled distributor points; 18-mm. Turbo-Action spark plugs; battery is 54-plate, 40 amp-hr on Sixes; 54-plate, 55 amp-hr on V-8's; fully aluminized muffler, tailpipe; positive crankcase emission control. All engines electronically mass-balanced for extra smoothness.

CLUTCH AND MANUAL TRANSMISSIONS: Non-centrifugal clutch with Sixes; semi-centrifugal clutch with V-8's. Face diameter 8½" with Sixes, 10" with V-8's. **3-Speed Manual Transmission** (standard with Sixes). Anti-friction bearings throughout. Forged bronze synchronizers in 2nd and direct. Shift lever on steering column. Ratios (to 1): 1st 3.29, 2nd 1.83, direct 1.00, rev. 4.46. **New Synchro-Smooth Drive** (standard with V-8's) with synchronized manual shifting in all three forward speeds. Ratios (to 1): 1st 2.79, 2nd 1.70, direct 1.00, rev. 2.87. **4-Speed Manual** (opt.) has floor-mounted "short stick" shift lever.

All forward gears synchronized for fast, smooth shifting. Ratios (to 1): Sixes—1st 3.16, 2nd 2.21, 3rd 1.41, direct 1.00, reverse 3.35; V-8's—1st 2.73, 2nd 2.04, 3rd 1.51, direct 1.00, reverse 2.81.

FORDOMATIC DRIVE (optional with all engines): Simplified design, lightweight cast-aluminum construction, minimum servicing. Torque converter in combination with planetary gear set. Vacuum-controlled throttle valve for smoothness, minimum servicing. Gear ratios (to 1): low 1.82, direct 1.00, reverse 1.73; converter (stall) 2.4 (Sixes), 2.05 (V-8's). In "D" range gives brisk, smooth starts in low. Effective engine braking in "L" position. Selector lever and quadrant on steering column, sequence P-R-N-D-L.

REAR AXLE: Semi-floating type with offset hypoid gears. Straddle-mounted drive pinion with V-8's. Induction-hardened forged shafts with permanently lubricated wheel bearings. **Axle Ratios** (to 1): **Sedans**—**144 Six:** 3.10 (3.50 opt.) with 3- or 4-speed manuals; 3.50 (3.10 opt.) with Fordomatic. **170 Six:** 3.20 (3.50 opt.) with 3-speed manual or Fordomatic; 3.50 (3.20 opt.) with 4-speed manual. **260 V-8:** 3.25 all transmissions. **Hardtops**—Same as Sedans; all engines and transmissions. **Convertibles**—**170 Six:** 3.50 (3.20 opt.) all transmissions. **260 V-8:** 3.25 all transmissions. **Wagons**—**144 Six:** 3.50 (4.00 opt.) all transmissions. **170 Six:** 3.50 all transmissions. **260 V-8:** 3.25 all transmissions.

FRONT SUSPENSION: Angle-Poised Ball-Joint type with coil springs pivot-mounted on upper arms. 36,000-mile lubrication intervals. Strut-stabilized lower arms. Threaded, permanently lubricated bushings in upper arms and rubber bushings in lower arms for softer ride. Built-in anti-dive control. Internally mounted hydraulic double-acting shock absorbers with rebound cutoff. Link-type rubber-bushed ride stabilizer. Tapered roller wheel bearings with 24,000-mile lubrication interval.

REAR SUSPENSION: Longitudinal, semi-elliptic leaf springs with rubber-bushed supports and compression-type shackles, giving variable-rate characteristics for a softer, more levelized ride. Asymmetrical design with rear axle located forward from center of springs for anti-squat control on take-off. Full-length liners between leaves —no lubrication required. Diagonally mounted double-acting shock absorbers.

STEERING: Magic-Circle low-friction recirculating-ball type steering gear provides easy handling. Anti-friction bearings throughout. Permanently lubricated steering linkage joints. Over-all steering ratio: 27 to 1 (manual or power steering). Turning diameter 38.8 feet.

BRAKES: Self-adjusting, double-sealed, self-energizing hydraulic with composite drums. Diameter, front and rear: 9 in. (Sixes), 10 in. (V-8's). Molded linings for long life and fade resistance. Total lining area (sq. in.): Six-cylinder models—Sedans 131; Hardtops, Convertibles and Wagons 157. V-8 models 154.

TIRES: Soft-Tread design, black, tubeless with Tyrex Rayon cord, safety-type rims. Six-cylinder models: Sedans—6.00 x 13, Others 6.50 x 13. V-8 models: Sedans & Hardtops—6.50 x 13, Others 7.00 x 13. Spare wheel and tire location: Wagons—cargo area behind right-hand wheelhousing; Other models—luggage compartment.

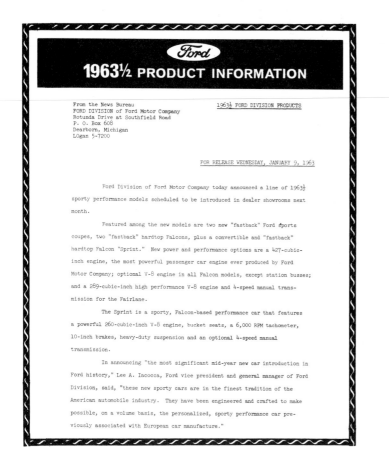

1963½ PRODUCT INFORMATION

From the News Bureau
FORD DIVISION of Ford Motor Company
Rotunda Drive at Southfield Road
P. O. Box 608
Dearborn, Michigan
LOgan 5-7200

1963½ FORD DIVISION PRODUCTS

FOR RELEASE WEDNESDAY, JANUARY 9, 1963

Ford Division of Ford Motor Company today announced a line of 1963½ sporty performance models scheduled to be introduced in dealer showrooms next month.

Featured among the new models are two new "fastback" Ford sports coupes, two "fastback" hardtop Falcons, plus a convertible and "fastback" hardtop Falcon "Sprint." New power and performance options are a 427-cubic-inch engine, the most powerful passenger car engine ever produced by Ford Motor Company; optional V-8 engine in all Falcon models, except station busses; and a 289-cubic-inch high performance V-8 engine and 4-speed manual transmission for the Fairlane.

The Sprint is a sporty, Falcon-based performance car that features a powerful 260-cubic-inch V-8 engine, bucket seats, a 6,000 RPM tachometer, 10-inch brakes, heavy-duty suspension and an optional 4-speed manual transmission.

In announcing "the most significant mid-year new car introduction in Ford history," Lee A. Iacocca, Ford vice president and general manager of Ford Division, said, "these new sporty cars are in the finest tradition of the American automobile industry. They have been engineered and crafted to make possible, on a volume basis, the personalized, sporty performance car previously associated with European car manufacture."

On Wednesday morning, January 9, 1963, Ford released information regarding their new Sprint Hardtop and Convertible.

Sprint windshield slants more sharply than Sedans, roofline is thinner in appearance.

1963½ Type 63C Sprint Har

13" wirewheel type Wheel Covers are standard on Sprint models; optional on others.

Mr. & Mrs. Swede Anderson, San Diego, California

New grill features horizontally accentuated lines.

F-O-R-D block letters are unchanged.

"Ornament" is actually formed and painted section at grill lower center.

Headlight bezel resembles 1962 style (page 74) but differs due to shape of grill.

Parking light lens is now amber, replacing the white 1962 lens.

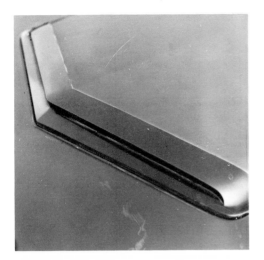

Bright-metal ornament, as used in 1962, is continued on the hood.

"Futura Spear" is standard on those models and Sprints.

Front fender ornaments are left- and right-handed. Standard on all Futura and Sprints, they are options on the basic Sedans.

Sprint script appears on front fender of those models. Most did also show the new special V-8 engine emblem, but a relatively few were built early in the year with the SIX.

Radio antenna is mount-
ed on right front fender.

Windshield wiper arms are unchanged.

Futura Hardtop and Convertible models also
have a different vent window assembly due to
the different angle of the windshield.

Sedan windshields are unchanged, but Convertible and Futura
Hardtops share new, larger glass.

The Futura fender ornament and side stripe are unique to that line.

Unique Sprint roof quarter emblem appears on Hardtop.

Cars built prior to 3/11/63 were provided with black inside door lock knobs (left) as used since 1960. After that, a new color-coded knob (above) appeared.

The rear quarter windows of the Hardtop will rotate to a fully retracted position.

Convertible and Hardtop have unique outside door handles different from other models which continue the 1960 handle.

"Futura" front fender ornament and side spear continue on side panels of the Sprint Convertible and Hardtop.

Rear deck ornament conceals keylock which is reached by lifting lower edge of ornament.

On most Futura models, lettering at the rear reads F-U-T-U-R-A. 2-door and 4-door Sedans, Type 76B Convertible with bucket seats, and Type 63C Futura Hardtop with bench seat all use letters F-A-L-C-O-N.

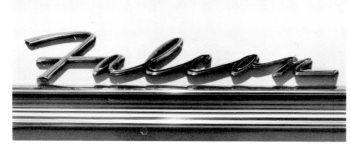

Familiar chromed Falcon script emblem appears on rear fenders.

Taillight is protected by overhang of fender and wrapped bumper.

For the first time, integrated optional back-up lights are placed at center of lens.

New radially-ringed taillight bezel appears for 1963.

Chrome finish gas cap is standard Falcon cap. Station wagons, Ranchero, and Sedan Delivery use different cap (page 136). Standard 2- and 4-Door Sedans use 1960 style (page 36).

Rear bumper is unchanged since 1960 model.

Sprint Hardtop and Convertible display F-A-L-C-O-N at the rear, not F-U-T-U-R-A.

Inside window crank is unchanged
from 1960.

Inside door handle continues unchanged.

The 1963 "Futura" arm rests appear in all models except the
Sedans and Wagons including Ranchero with standard trim (page
143).

Data Plate continues on left front door. Body
identification of 63C identifies Sprint Hardtop.

1963 4-door panel shown for comparison.

Sprint Hardtop door displays its deluxe trim.

Simulated holes dress up the three spokes of the Sprint wheel.

Special Sprint 16" steering wheel has wood-grained rim.

Sprint tachometer mounts at the top center of instrument panel and is standard in the Sprint models.

Hub of the Sprint steering wheel is clearly lettered.

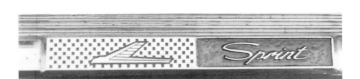

Sprint emblem appears on glove compartment trim of those models.

1963 Futura models have a full-width dress-up chromed plastic trim on the instrument panel. Tachometer is standard on Sprint. A similar model is optional on others.

Hardtop dome light has chromed plastic bezel.

Rear seat arm rests with ash trays appear in Hardtop.

Front seat backs of standard Sprint bucket seats fold nicely out of the way to allow excellent accessibility to rear seats.

Redesigned chromed center clip serves to secure inside corners of sun visors. Inside windshield moldings are fully chromed in Futura Hardtop models and Sprints.

New chromed "Floating" rear view mirror is a feature of Sprint and Futura Hardtops and Convertibles.

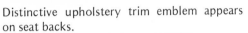

Distinctive upholstery trim emblem appears on seat backs.

Bench-type rear seat is upholstered to resemble the front bucket seats.

All-vinyl bucket seat has horizontally-striped insert with surrounding bolster on back.

Sides of console are color-keyed to upholstery.

Sprint model is provided with a standard between-the-seats chromed console.

New instrument panel mask and dial changes appearance of panel.

Shape of instrument cluster is unchanged, but new Falcon insignia at lower center quickly identifies 1963.

White gear shift lever knob continues.

Fuel (and temperature) instruments are revised (compare page 82).

OIL (and GEN) lights are continued.

New push-button radio has revised dial layout and narrower push-buttons than earlier style (page 81).

There is no change in ignition switch.

A new temperature indicating meter is used and dresses up the 1963 Instrument Panel. (compare page 82).

Function of GEN light is unchanged.

Optional Falcon Fordomatic transmission can be "kicked down" for passing at speeds up to 50 mph!

Deluxe interior trim of the Futuras includes white knobs with chromed inserts.

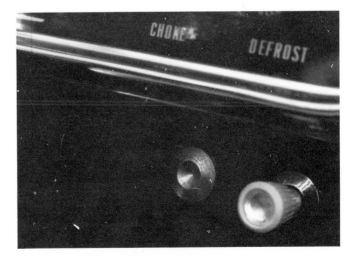

Installation of V-8 with its automatic choke eliminates the need for a choke knob which is then blanked off. Lettering, however, still appears on panel above it.

The luggage space of the Falcon Hardtop is 25.9 cubic feet. The Convertible, due to its folding top mechanism has less, 18.7 cubic feet.

Latch, on under side of trunk lid, is released by key lock under deck lid emblem (page 102).

The catch for deck lid latch is placed on rear panel and can be adjusted for proper alignment. Note Burtex trunk mat used in Futura models.

Spare wheel is secured in horizontal position at forward right corner.

Sprint decal identifies valve covers used on the engines in Sprint models.

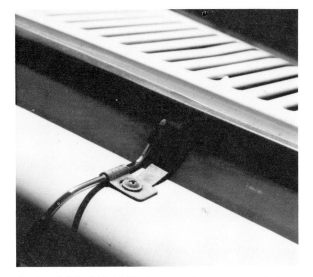

Optional Windshield Washer nozzles are concealed under rear lip of hood and direct water through the cowl air intake onto the windshield.

Decal is affixed to left-side valve cover at its forward end.

The "two" optional V-8 engines offered in 1963 are alike except that the Sprint 260 V-8 is dressed up with chromed air cleaner, oil filler cap, and valve covers.

Data Plate identifies the Sprint Convertible as a Type 76B. However, "ordinary" Futura Convertible with six cylinder engine (page 118) and optional bucket seats is also a Type 76B.

1963 Type 76B Sprint Convertible

Introduced in January of 1963, the Sprint Convertible and Sprint Hardtop were the top of the Falcon line for the year. Although some few Sprint models were built with six-cylinder engines, from that time on the Sprint Option include as standard a 260 cubic inch "Sprint V-8". Other items included as standard equipment included a courtesy light under the Instrument Panel for the Convertible (dome light in the Hardtop), color-keyed carpets, front and rear; color-keyed windshield Garnish Moldings, Instrument Panel and Steering Column.

Popular accessories include a 4-speed manual transmission; Ford Air Conditioner (un-available with 4-speed option); color-keyed Padded Instrument Panel (installed during production unless omission was specified); Power Steering, Backup Lights, Etc.)

Mr. & Mrs. Bill Anderson, San Diego, California

Convertible roof extends forward to seal at top of windshield frame.

Sprint Convertibles and Hardtops have a side trim unique to those two models. Sprint side trim is chromed; other Futura models' side trim insert is painted either white or black.

This chromed Sprint emblem appears on the front fenders.

Virtually all 1963 Sprint models included a Standard V-8 engine whose presence was noted by this emblem.

Both of the emblems shown in above photographs are mounted in the front fender insets; their relative positions are reversed on right fender.

Large Convertible rear window is made of clear vinyl and folds easily with top. A power-operated top is standard on all 1963 Falcon Convertibles.

Sprint, a top-line version of the Futura models, bears the name F-A-L-C-O-N on the rear.

A bright-metal rocker panel molding is standard on Sprint models and is available as an Option on others.

Rear seats are upholstered to suggest bucket seating, but will accommodate three adults.

Front bucket seats and center console are standard in all Sprint models, Futura Sports Hardtop and Sports Convertible.

Convertible rear seat is slightly narrower than that in Hardtop due to need for space of the Folding Top mechanism. Ash trays are located in top surface of integral arm rests.

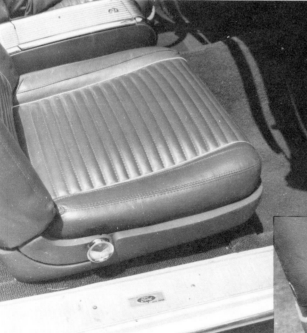

Convertible seat hinges differ from those used in Hardtop (page 106).

Door sill plate now bears a new Ford script label with black background.

116

The sun visors used in Convertibles have a curved cross-section which enables them to serve additionally as wind deflectors when top is lowered.

The Sprint tachometer and Sprint name on glove box are standard for those models.

An accessory non-glare inside rear view mirror has rocker-arm DAY/NIGHT control.

1963

Convertible tops were offered in White, Black, or Blue.

The Futura Convertible and the Futura Sports Convertible are furnished with Futura Full Wheel Covers although optional Wire Wheel Covers (page 295) were a popular Option.

White top was particularly attractive with darker color cars.

In addition to the relatively well known Sprint Convertible, the Falcon line for 1963 included two more similar models. The Type 76A Futura Convertible was the basic model and appeared with Futura trim items and bench seats. The 101 horsepower Special Six was standard.

An interesting alternate was the Type 76B (same as Sprint) Futura Sports Convertible which had a standard Bucket Seat interior.

The Challenger 260 V-8 (without the Sprint chrome trim) was an available Option for either, as was the 4-speed manual transmission; Simulated Wire Wheel Covers; White Sidewall Tires; Padded Instrument Panel; and Bright-Metal Rocker Panel Moldings.

1963 Type 76B Futura Sports Convertible   *Mr. & Mrs. Paul Young, Leucadia, California*

Absence of tachometer is obvious difference in views of Futura Convertibles (above) and Sprint (page 117).

All Convertible models shared same windshield; height is slightly less than Hardtop to allow for folding top header plate.

Fender top ornaments are standard on all Convertibles.

Black Futura Sports Convertible has white-painted insert in side stripe.

Compared to Sprint fender (page 114) the Futura Convertible lacks both Sprint and V-8 engine emblems.

Chromed fuel cap is continued on Futura models.

Lettered F-U-T-U-R-A appears at rear; Sprint models (page 102) have F-A-L-C-O-N. Coincidence of six-letter words makes for Production simplicity.

Backup lights are a popular Option.

Convertible rear window is clear vinyl and folds with top.

Futura Convertible (Type 76A) has standard interior and color-keyed Steering Wheel with bright-metal horn button at hub.

The horn "button" is actually black-painted center of a one-piece bright-metal hub cover.

Futura Sports Convertible (Type 76B) has a chromed horn ring to dress up its color-keyed three-spoke steering wheel.

Futura Sports Convertible has Futura deluxe Interior, and features standard bucket seats and center console.

Knobs on all Convertibles are white with chromed centers.

Futura trim plate appears on glove box in place of appropriate Sprint identification on that model (page 105).

Futura Sports Convertible has deluxe interior trim as does the Sprint.

Convertible bucket seats differ from those used in Hardtops. Hinge in Convertible has chromed knob (above); Hardtop hinge has extended chrome molding (page 106). Convertible bucket seats are also used in the Super Deluxe Squire Wagon (Type 71D).

Two chromed latches on Convertible windshield headers release top for folding.

The chromed top latches are concealed behind the sun visors which must be moved to release them. Note Standard transmission is 3-speed manual; optional Fordomatic is shown here.

Optional 4-speed transmission shift pattern is displayed in top of shift lever knob.

Futura Sports Convertible has standard bucket seat interior with a Console. The 4-speed Manual Transmission however is an Option.

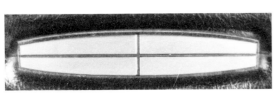

Seat back emblems are chromed inserts.

Convertible rear seat ash trays are recessed into a trim panel placed around the folding top mechanism.

Contrasting metallic piping highlights the bucket-styled rear seat upholstery of Futura rear seats.

All convertibles were provided with a standard Power-Operated top. Colors available were White, Blue, or Black. With the top down and the boot installed, the Convertible was truly a sporty and youthful model. With top up and latched and windows up the Convertible became a closed and weathertight car.

This switch, located on left side of instrument panel controls the Power-Operated Convertible Top.

Color-keyed top boot is installed over lowered Top both to protect and also to display more attractive appearance.

Futura Sedans and Hardtops have distinctive
"Gold" Falcon emblem on the rear roof pillars.

1963 Type 63C Futura Sports Coupe

Rear panel displays F-U-T-U-R-A in block letters.

The mid-year Futura Hardtop bench seat model was also offered as a Futura Sports Coupe (as well as a Sprint Hardtop). The Sports Coupe had the standard SIX, but optional 170 cu. in. Special SIX or the Challenger 260 V-8 were available Options. Its principal upgrade was a standard bucket seat interior with its center-mounted Console. Futura Full Wheel Covers were standard, but Wire Wheel Covers (page 295) were also a popular Option.

Mr. Tony DeJesus, Oceanside, California

The side trim insert of the Futura models (other than Sprint) is painted White, Red, or Black. Sprint is all bright.

The "Futura Spear" on those models other than the Sprint has inserts painted Black, White, or Red. Sprint model spear differs, having a bright finish to match its distinctive side trim.

Bright-metal rocker panel moldings, standard on the Sprint models, are an available accessory for the others.

Futura Sports Coupe is an upgraded Futura Hardtop, but has no special external identifying features.

Conventional Falcon chromed script appears on rear fenders.

Futura Hardtop and Futura Sports Coupe have exactly the same exterior, differing only in use of bucket seats and console in Sports Coupe.

Futura Sports Coupe has the deluxe door panels found in other Futura models.

Hardtops have slightly wide rear seats and separate arm rests with integral ash trays provided.

Bucket seats with center console and bucket-styled rear seat cushions are standard in Futura Sports Coupe.

Sports Coupe has the deluxe Futura trim across its instrument panel. Although a tachometer is not standard equipment in this model, it was available as an Accessory. Such a unit would have the "Rotunda" name rather than Sprint identification.

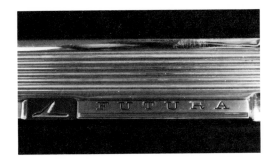

As in Futura models other than Sprints, the Futura name appears in the glove box trim.

Introduced as a 1963 Accessory was an interesting High Performance Kit for the 170 SIX engine. Consisting of a revised cam and valve train; increased capacity fuel system; special distributor and revised cylinder head, it also included a heavy duty drive shaft.

PART NO. C2DZ 6B068-A

170 HIGH PERFORMANCE KIT

The completeness of this high performance Falcon Kit adds sparked performance to the 170 Falcon engine. It provides durability during sustained high-speed highway driving. This kit offers that "extra punch" when needed for passing and attaining higher top speeds.

1963

Two Sales Folders were issued for the 1963 Ranchero. Virtually identical, the later issue, dated 2/63, first offered the 164 horsepower 260 V-8 engine as an available Option.

Owner's Manual for Ranchero is identical to those supplied with other models of the Falcon line.

Front fender ornaments are a dress-up Accessory not normally found on Rancheros.

1963 Type 66B Deluxe Ranchero

A "new Model", the Type 66B was first offered for 1963. Fundamentally merely a Type 66A Standard Ranchero with the Deluxe Trim Option, it was furnished the new designation for the first time, having previously been known simply as a "Type 66A Ranchero with Deluxe Trim Package".

Type 66B Ranchero has bright-metal trim on cab back and window frames; similar Type 66A Ranchero parts are painted body color. The door edge guards are an Option.

Mrs. Dorothy Angiolet, Encinitas, California

1963

Doors and rear quarter for 1963 are unchanged. Doors are same as style introduced in 1960 although fenders differ.

Fuel Filler Cap on 1960/63 Ranchero is round and has rectangular knob.

1960-1963 models used same tailgate with F-O-R-D block letters unchanged in 1962/63 and Ranchero emblem same from 1960-63.

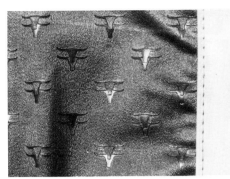

Again the "Western Motif" steerhead patterned beige vinyl with light beige bolsters was standard. The Type 66B Deluxe Ranchero offered a choice of all black or all red pleated vinyl upholstery with matching bolsters and surrounding areas.

The three-spoke steering wheel in black or red, with a horn ring was supplied in the 66B Deluxe Ranchero. Note that instrument panel lacks the dress up Futura chrome trim (page 133).

1963 Deluxe Ranchero, Type 66B uses this door panel.

The seat is bench type; divided back; either side folding forward for storage access behind seat. Deluxe upholstery shown.

1963

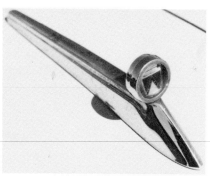

Fender top ornaments are standard on the Deluxe wagons, but are not used on the standard versions.

This 4-door wagon is a Deluxe as indicated by its side stripe.

Wagons use same hood as other models.

1963 Type 71B Falcon 4-door Deluxe Wagon

The optional V-8, available in all Wagon models, is indicated by emblem on front fender.

1963 Type 59A Falcon 2-door Wag

A one-piece emblem-stripe is used on the Deluxe Wagons.

The standard 2- and 4-door Wagon's 5½" emblem together with the chromed Falcon script are also used on the 2- and 4-door standard Sedans.

Mr. Alfred Ybarra, Lake San Marcos, California

Mr. Keith Miller, Sebastopol, California

Rear quarter windows are alike, but standard Wagon rear corners are painted body color.

Deluxe Wagons have stainless steel rear quarter post trim.

Falcon script on front fenders of standard Wagons (preceeding page) is moved to rear quarter on Deluxe Wagons.

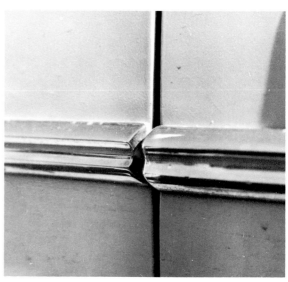

Cross section of 1963 dress-up trim differs from 1962 (page 77).

Deluxe Wagons and Sedans have length-of-body trim stripes.

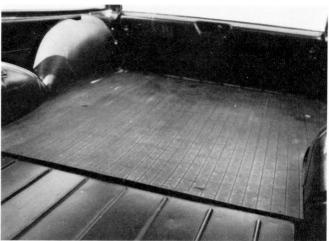

Rear door windows in 4-door Wagons are divided into a rearward stationary pane and a forward section which can be lowered.

The Wagon floor is grooved for rigidity. A rubber pad is supplied from the rear seat back to protect the cargo floor.

A latch on the right rear wheel housing holds the folding rear seat in erect position.

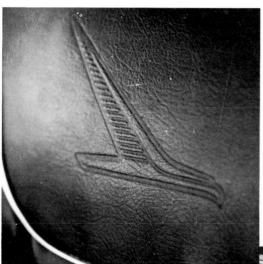

Falcon emblem is embossed into center of rear seat back.

Deluxe Wagon interiors are offered in three all-vinyl and a wide selection of vinyl/cloth choices.

1960-63 rear bumper is alike on all models.

An Optional Power Tailgate Window operator provides key-opening at the rear and a switch on the instrument panel.

The tailgate inner panel is grooved for strength and extends the cargo floor area when lowered.

Tailgate window crank has keylock at its hub.

F-A-L-C-O-N appears in block letters on Wagon tailgates.

Tailgate is counterbalanced for ease and has integral folding hinges.

Wagons and Sedans have suspended mirrors. Note use of two visors, standard in all models except Sedan Delivery.

This is the "standard" door panel for 1963. Note simplified arm rests rather than dressed up "Futura" style (page 104).

With rear seat and tailgate lowered, Falcon Wagons offer over 105 inches of load length.

Deluxe Wagons have bright-metal trim at side windows.

FALCON for '64
The Total Performance Compact

Type 54A 4-Door Sedan (Bench)
54B Futura 4-Door Sedan
54D 4-Door Sedan (Deluxe)
59A 2-Door Station Wagon
62A 2-Door Sedan (Bench)
62B Futura 2-Door Sedan (Bench)
62C 2-Door Sedan (Bucket)
62D 2-Door Sedan (Deluxe-Bench)
63B Futura 2-Door Hardtop (Bench)
63C 2-Door Hardtop (6 cyl-Bucket)
63D 2-Door Hardtop (8 cyl-Bucket)
63E 2-Door Hardtop (8 cyl-Bucket)
63H Futura 2-Door Hardtop (Bucket)
66A Ranchero (Bench)
66B Deluxe Ranchero (Bench)
66H Deluxe Ranchero (Bucket)
71A 4-Door Station Wagon
71B Futura 4-Door Station Wagon
71C 4-Door Squire
76A Convertible (6 cyl-Bench)
76B Convertible (6 cyl-Bucket)
76D Futura Convertible (8 cyl-Bucket)
76E Futura Convertible (8 cyl-Bench)
78A Sedan Delivery
78B Deluxe Sedan Delivery
89B Club Wagon
89D Deluxe Club Wagon
89C Station Bus

Options:
Fordomatic Drive or 4-Speed Manual Transmission
Padded Instrument Panel & visors
Seat Belts
Wagon Roof Rack
Deluxe Wheel Covers
Remote Control Outside Mirror
Electric Clock
Ford Air Conditioner
Power Steering
Power Brakes
Courtesy Light Group
   includes lights for ash tray, glove box, trunk (cargo
      area in Wagons), map light, backup lights,
      front & rear courtesy switches (all available
      separately).
All-Transistor Radio
Spotlight with Mirror
StudioSonic Sound System

Convertible Tonneau Cover
Two-Tone Paint
Tinted Glass
White Sidewall Tires
Windshield Washer & 2-speed Electric Wipers
Conventional Rear Seat Speakers
Vinyl Roof (Hardtops)
Pleated vinyl trim (Futura sedans)
Inside Non-Glare mirror; Parking Brake Warning Light;
   Glove Box Lock; Remote-Control Trunk Release; Rocker
   Panel Molding; Door Edge Guards; Fresh Air Heater (installed
   unless a delete Option);
Power Tailgate Window (standard on Squire);
170 Special SIX engine
164-hp Challenger 260 V-8
164-hp Sprint 260 V-8 (standard on Sprints) — same as
   Challenger 260 V-8 plus special trim items, air cleaner
   and muffler
Other Items

See our big blue picnic machine. It's a Falcon. Daddy says it has total performance—refined and perfected in open competition—and the freshest look in compacts. On weekends, its big 260 V-8 takes you to wonderful places. But I should warn you: on weekdays it may take you to school!

FORD

1964 saw a major change in appearance as Falcon bodies lost their rounded lines and saw the introduction of new more linear styling. A new 116-hp Falcon 200 Special SIX engine was introduced as an available Wagon Option, but other engine choices were unchanged.

By now, Falcon was offering not only economy, but also style, comfort, and "the plushest ride ever built into a compact car". Top of the line were the Sprint Convertible and Hardtop which included the Sprint 260 V-8; Wire Wheel Covers; Special Steering Wheel; Bright-Metal Rocker Panel Moldings; bucket seats and console, and some special "Sprint" emblems all as standard.

The Futura Sedans were the dressed up versions of the Falcon Sedans, and the Futura Hardtops and Convertibles were the basic platform for the Sprint models. In all, there were 28 distinct Body Type numbers assigned and their Sales Folder claimed merely that there were 17 new models for the year.

1964 FALCON SPECIFICATIONS

COLOR AND UPHOLSTERY SELECTIONS: You have a choice of 11 '64 Falcon single tone colors or 12 two-tone combinations in durable, brilliant Diamond Lustre Enamel. There are 26 upholstery choices: 8 cloth and vinyl combinations (6 std., 2 opt.), 15 all-vinyl trims in Wagons, Convertibles and Hardtops; plus 3 all-vinyl options in Futura Sedans. Your Ford Dealer will be happy to show you actual samples of '64 Falcon colors and upholsteries.

FALCON DESIGN: Among many Falcon feature highlights are: Welded Integral Body and Frame (quietness, high strength-to-weight ratio); Body Fully Insulated and Weather-Sealed; Parallel Action Electric Windshield Wipers; Deep-Dish Steering Wheel; Dual Sun Visors with Retention Clips; Safety-Yoke Door Latches; Front Seat Belt Anchors; Center-Fill Fueling (sedans); Counterbalanced Hood and Deck Lid (sedans), Tailgate (wagons); Lined Trunk (sedans); Vinyl-Coated Rubber Cargo Mat (wagons); 20-Gal. Fuel Tank (V-8 wagons), 14-Gal. (all others); Roll-Down Tailgate Window (wagons); Quick-Converting Second Seat Providing Flat, Level Loadspace (wagons); Upright Spare Tire Stowage (wagons).

TWICE-A-YEAR (OR 6,000-MILE) MAINTENANCE: The 1964 Falcon goes 36,000 miles (or 3 years) between major chassis lubes; 6,000 miles (or 6 months) between oil changes and minor lubes. In fact, Falcon needs so little service it's just good sense to see that it gets the best—at your Ford Dealer's. His factory-trained mechanics and special tools add up to a great service combination you can get nowhere else! Other savings include: engine coolant-antifreeze, installed at the factory, good for 36,000 miles (or two years); self-adjusting brakes; aluminized muffler; and galvanized vital underbody parts to resist rust and corrosion.

ENGINES: 85-hp Falcon Six (std. on all except Futura Convertibles, Sprints and Wagons)—144 cu. in. displ.; 3.50" bore x 2.50" stroke; 8.7 to 1 comp. ratio; reg. fuel; single-barrel carb; manual choke; self-adj. valves with hydraulic lifters; oil cap'y, with filter change, 4.5 qt.

101-hp Falcon 170 Special Six (std. on Futura Convertibles, opt. required installed in production on Wagons, opt. on other models except Sprints)—170 cu. in. displ.; 3.50" bore x 2.94" stroke. Other specs. same as above.

116-hp Falcon 200 Special Six (opt. on Wagons)—200 cu. in. displ.; 3.68" bore x 3.13" stroke. Other specifications same as Falcon Six above.

164-hp Challenger 260 V-8 (opt. except Sprints)—260 cu. in. displ.; 3.80" bore x 2.87" stroke; 8.8 to 1 comp. ratio; reg. fuel; 2-barrel carb.; new vacuum-piston-operated automatic choke; self-adj. valves with hydraulic lifters; oil cap'y, with filter change, 5 qt.

164-hp Sprint 260 V-8 (std. on Sprints)—same as Challenger 260 V-8 plus special trim items, power-toned air cleaner and muffler.

ENGINE FEATURES: For more economy and longer life Falcon engines have short-stroke, low-friction design; 6,000-mile (or 6-month) full-flow disposable-type oil filter; 36,000-mile (or 3-year) disposable-type fuel filter and replaceable dry-type element air cleaner. 190° thermostat; 12-volt electrical system; weatherproof ignition; battery 54-plate: 40 amp-hr (Sixes)—55 amp-hr (V-8's); fully aluminized muffler and tailpipe; crankcase emission control system. All engines electronically mass-balanced for operating smoothness.

CLUTCH AND MANUAL TRANSMISSIONS: Non-centrifugal clutch with Sixes; semi-centrifugal clutch with V-8's. Face diameter 8½" with Sixes, 10" with V-8's.

3-Speed Transmission (std. on Sixes except 200 Special Six) has forged bronze synchronizers in 2nd and direct for smooth operation. Anti-friction bearings throughout. Standard "H" shift pattern with lever on steering column. **Synchro-Smooth Drive Transmission** (std. on V-8's) synchronized manual shifting in all three forward gears; clash-free downshifting to low while under way. **4-Speed Transmission** (opt. on all models except Wagons) with floor-mounted stick shift. All forward gears synchronized for fast, smooth shifting.

FORDOMATIC DRIVE (opt. on all engines): Features simplified design, lightweight cast-aluminum construction, vacuum-controlled throttle valve for greater smoothness, less servicing. Torque converter in combination with compound planetary gear set. In "D" range gives brisk, smooth starts in low. Effective engine braking in "L" position. Selector lever and quadrant on steering column, sequence P-R-N-D-L.

REAR AXLE: Semi-floating type with deep-offset hypoid gears. Induction-hardened forged shafts with permanently lubricated wheel bearings.

FRONT SUSPENSION: Angle-Poised Ball-Joint type with coil springs pivot-mounted on upper arms. 36,000-mile (or 3-year) lube intervals. Strut-stabilized lower arms with larger bushings. Threaded, permanently lubricated bushings in upper arms and low-friction rubber bushings in lower arms for softer, smoother ride. Link-type, rubber-bushed ride stabilizer. Built-in anti-dive control. Tapered roller wheel bearings. Double-acting shock absorbers with stable-viscosity fluid.

REAR SUSPENSION: Asymmetrical, variable-rate design with rear axle located forward from center of springs for anti-squat on take-off. Longer, wider leaf-type springs with tip inserts and wide spring base provide a softer, more stable, levelized ride. Diagonally mounted double-acting shock absorbers with stable-viscosity fluid.

STEERING: Recirculating-ball type steering gear provides easy handling. Anti-friction bearings throughout. Permanently lubricated steering linkage joints. Over-all steering ratio: 27 to 1. Turning diameter: 38.8 feet.

BRAKES: Self-adjusting, self-energizing design. Diameter, front and rear: 9 in. (Sixes), 10 in. (V-8's). Molded linings for longer life and fade resistance. Total lining area (sq. in.) (Sixes)—Sedans & Hardtops 131; Convertibles & Wagons 157. All V-8 models 154.

TIRES: Soft-Tread design, black, tubeless with Tyrex rayon cord. Safety-type rims. (Sixes): Sedans—6.00 x 13; other models—6.50 x 13. (V-8's): Sedans and Hardtops—6.50 x 13, others 7.00 x 13.

1964 Type 76D Sprint Convertible

Sprint Hardtop data plate shows Body Type 63D (2-Door Hardtop 8 cyl-Bucket).

1964 Type 63D Sprint Hardtop

Sprint Convertible data plate shows
Body Type 76D (Futura Convertible 8 cyl-bucket).

The 1964 Sprint Convertible and Hardtop featured the 164 hp Sprint V-8 (with chromed engine dressup); Synchro-Smooth 3-speed manual transmission; Wire Wheel Covers; Bright-metal Rocker Panel Moldings; Bucket Seats and Console; Sports-Type Steering Wheel; Tachometer; etc. Popular Options included Fordomatic or 4-Speed Manual Transmission; Power Brakes (only with Fordomatic); Power Steering; Padded Instrument Panel; Radio; Seat Belts, etc.

Mr. & Mrs. Ken Overmiller
Spring Valley, California

Mr. & Mrs. Richard Noonan, Carlsbad, California

Polished aluminum bezels are removed to re-place or re-position the headlamp.

New grill for 1964 displays rectangular blocks with "floating" dividers.

Amber parking light lens, introduced in 1963, is continued.

New front bumper for 1964 is now more massive, and has a strengthening "rib" along its lower edge (compare page 98).

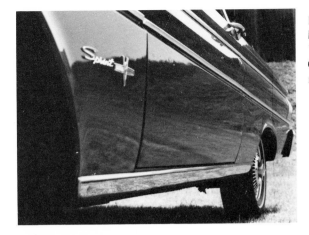

Bright-metal Rocker Panel Moldings are standard on all 1964 Futura Hardtops and Convertibles (includes Sprint models).

The frames of the Futura Hardtops and Convertibles (Types 63 and 76) were reinforced at rear of front wheel wells with a formed gusset (below and left). This was later extended to all cars factory-equipped with a V-8 engine. Other models did not include this feature (right).

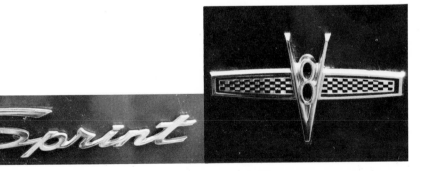

Chromed Sprint script and V-8 emblem are standard on fender flanks. V-8 emblem is unique to Sprint; others used emblem on page 190 when appropriate.

Bright-metal side trim and rear "chevrons" are standard on all Futura models.

149

New hood has deep trough running full length at center.

New hood ornament is standard on all Futura models
and part of the upgrading Convenience Package on
Falcon Sedans.

New hood has sharply creased leading edge better to display lettering.

These block letters appear on front of 1964 hood. Despite similarity to 1962/63 style (page 75), they do differ in style.

Windshield glass is unchanged from 1963. Both clear and optional Tinted glass is offered.

Although appearing unchanged, there is actually a new outside door handle used in 1964. Note embossed mounting stands on the new 1964 door.

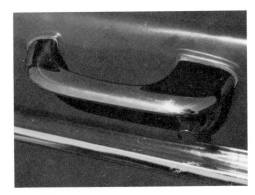

Outside keylock has changed from 1963 and earlier style (page 66).

Wire Wheel Covers are standard on Sprint models, optional on others.

Convertible's windshield header appears thin due to overhanging door section. Parallel-acting windshield wipers are continued on all models.

Hardtop windshield header trim appears to be wider as steel roof has thinner section.

Full-floating rear-view mirror with its base cemented to the windshield is exclusive to Futura Hardtop and Convertibles. Others use suspended type shown on page 143.

PRODUCT OF
Ford
MOTOR COMPANY

Ford script label appears on door sill scuff plate.

Falcon tachometers mount on instrument panel top surface near center.

Sprint tachometer is so indicated by script at upper center of dial face.

The tachometer is also available as an Option in other models. When so ordered, its has Rotunda logo rather than Sprint. All are calibrated to 6000 RPM.

New Safety-Yoke door latches are left- and right-handed and are so-stamped.

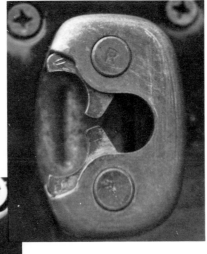

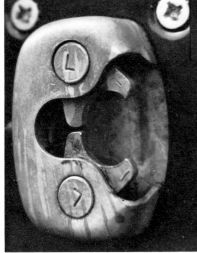

Either Safety-Yoke latch closes on this anvil. Note date stamped into face.

Rear window of Hardtop rotates into quarter when opened.

All Futura models have the side trim; only Sprints have fender emblems seen here. Others have Futura emblem (page 182).

Convertible's rear windows also rotate into quarter when lowered.

Convertible has trim rail at base of top on which snaps are provided for the attachment of boot when top is lowered.

New rear deck lid keylock appears relacing former emblem (page 115).

Despite Futura lineage, the lettering at rear of Sprint models reads F-A-L-C-O-N.

Sprint emblem appears in trim panel at rear on those models.

Chromed gas cap appears on all Futura models and Sprints.

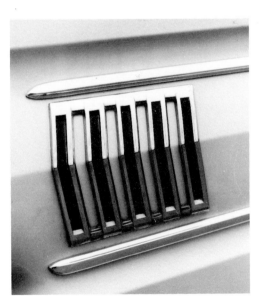

The interesting Chevron design is unique to the Futura models but also appears on the bucket-seated Deluxe Ranchero.

Well-defined rear luggage compartment holds 12.2 cubic feet of storage (9.1 in Convertible).

Rear window of Hardtop is framed in bright-metal trim.

Standard taillight lens is all-red plastic.

Backup light is an Option.

Optional backup light is placed in center of a two-part lens. Note FoMoCo. script at bottom of back-up light lens.

New seat back emblem appears for 1964 (see page 125).

Bucket seats are standard in Sprint Models, the Futura Sports Convertible, and the Type 66H Deluxe Ranchero.

Emblem appears only in center of rear seat back unlike 1963 where they were used in two places (page 125).

A new center console appears for 1964.

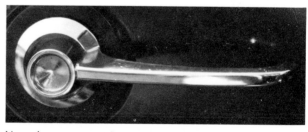

New shapes appear for both the inside door latch and the window riser handles (compare page 104).

Futura arm rests have chromed dress-up.

Center of steering wheel horn button assembly is clearly lettered.

Sprint steering wheel is simulated-wood rimmed, three-spoke, and with chromed horn button assembly.

Arms of the Sprint steering wheel horn button assembly have simulated holes, but these are actually black-painted depressions.

Suspended beneath instrument panel at left side is a lettered knob which controls incoming vent air.

Sprint emblems appear on the front doors of those models. Otherwise, similar Futura emblems (page 186) will appear.

Futura trim includes a painted and chromed plastic dress-up trim piece on the glove box door.

Suspended Falcon clutch and brake pedals have distinctive rubber pads.

Rear seats are upholstered to resemble the appearance of front buckets, but are actually a bench seat for three.

A two-tone interior is one of the five choices for Sprint models.

Despite literature indicating otherwise, this particular Sprint Hardtop (note emblem on door panel) apparently was never equipped with the "standard" tachometer.

1964

New color-keyed 2-spoke Safety-Type steering wheel with chromed horn ring is standard for Futura models.

Spokes extend beyond ring to provide comfortable activation of horn with thumb of either hand without removing hand from wheel.

A chromed horn button (without ring) is provided for standard installation in the Sedans and Wagons.

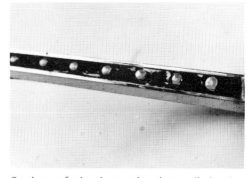

Spokes of the horn ring have distinctive raised rings.

Sedan and Wagon steering wheel is same as above but lacks horn ring assembly.

Turn signal and transmission shift lever knobs are white through 1963; from 1964 on, they are black.

1964 steering wheel horn button and horn ring assembly.

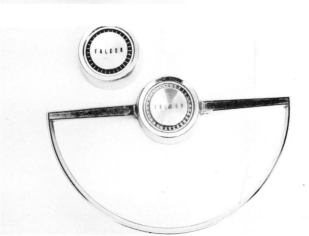

Sedan and Wagon interiors have standard painted instrument panel; only the Instrument Cluster has chromed plastic trim.

1960 Falcon 4-Door Wagon

1960 Falcon Fordor Sedan

1960 Falcon Tudor Sedan

1961 Falcon Ranchero

1961 Falcon Fordor Sedan

1962 Falcon Ranchero

1962 Falcon Sports Futura

1962 Falcon Tudor Sedan

1963 Falcon Sprint Hardtop

1963 Falcon Ranchero

1963 Falcon 4-Door Deluxe Wagon

1963 Falcon Futura Convertible

1963 Falcon Futura Sports Coupe

1963 Falcon Sprint Convertible

1964 Falcon Club Wagon

1964 Falcon Futura Hardtop

1964 Falcon Sprint Convertible

1964 Falcon (standard) Ranchero

1964 Falcon (deluxe) Ranchero

1964 Falcon Ranchero (deluxe with optional Body Side Trim)

1964 Falcon Sprint Hardtop

1965 Falcon Convertible (six cylinder)

1965 Falcon Convertible (with V-8 Option)

1965 Falcon Sedan Delivery

1965 Falcon Futura 4-Door Sedan

1965 Falcon Futura 2-Door Sedan

1965 Falcon Deluxe Ranchero (with two-tone paint Option)

1965 Falcon Squire Wagon

1965 Falcon Deluxe Ranchero with Optional Body Side Trim

1966 Falcon 4-Door Sedan

**1966 Ford Custom
Ranchero**

1967 Falcon Futura Wagon

1967 Fairlane Ranchero

1967 Falcon Futura 4-Door Sedan

1968 Falcon Club Coupe

1969 Futura Club Coupe

1968 Ranchero 500

1970 Falcon Futura Club Coupe

New speedometer for 1964 reads to an ambitious 120 MPH; earlier calibrations (page 123) read only to 100 MPH.

Standard instrument panel trim provides painted glove box door. Padded instrument panel is an Option.

Standard control knobs are all black.

Futura control knobs are black with chromed insert.

Optional all-transistor push-button radio is installed in center of instrument panel.

Six-cylinder engines require a manual choke control which is installed under the instrument panel at its far left. V-8 engines have automatic choke and this control is omitted.

Futura instrument panel trim is a set of four pieces of chromed-and-painted plastic extending across the full width of the panel.

Standard instrument panel has single painted-and-chromed Instrument Cluster.

Red lens in rectangular window is OIL warning.

Odometer is at center of Cluster.

GEN warning is illuminated if that unit fails.

A new switch appears as the Convertible power top control and is also used for Wagon Power Tailgate Window. This replaces earlier style (page 126).

Right edge of Futura instrument panel trim is squared off to mate with matching center section; both ends are rounded on standard trim piece (previous page).

New fuel gauge is dressed with center chrome; headlamp condition is indicated by HI BEAM light.

New matching temperature gauge is similarly trimmed. Both right- and left-turns are indicated by single TURN SIGNAL light.

Futura cigarette lighter is standard; the optional Falcon Sedan lighter would have all-black knob.

1964 radio has Civil Defense dial markings at 650 and 1250 KC.

Fresh Air Heater is installed in all models during production but can be omitted by exercising a special "delete" Option when ordering.

Ignition switch assembly is unchanged.

Futura Hardtops and Convertibles had inside rear view mirror cemented to windshield; a chromed center bracket at the header secures the inside ends of the visors.

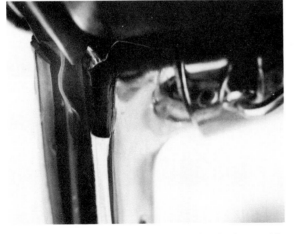

Apparent installation of notched Hardtop side chrome results in unsightly gap at upper corner of Convertible windshield frame.

Futura Hardtop and Convertible (but not Futura Sedans) have chromed inside windshield reveal moldings.

Challenger 260 V-8 has blue-painted air cleaner and valve covers; black oil filler cap.

Sprint 260 V-8 is same engine, but has chromed air cleaner, valve covers, and oil filler cap.

Falcon SIX and Special SIX also have painted accessories.

Heavy forge mounting bracket is needed for large generator supplied with the 260 engine.

1964 260 V-8 valve cover differs from 1963 style (page 111) as oil filler tube has been moved to forward part of left side cover.

Sprint decal, when applicable, is shifted to the rear end of left side valve cover.

The oil level dip stick for both Falcon V-8 engines is painted.

Distinctive Falcon emblem appears on fender flanks behind wheel well opening of Futura Hardtops, Convertibles, and Sedans other than the Sprint models.

The Futura 2-Door Sedan is a top-of-the-line version of the standard 2-Door. Distinctive for its use of Futura side trim and hood ornament, it also has bright-metal side window trim; full carpeting; arm rests and ash trays front and rear; Courtesy-lighted interiors; dual visors; and a cigarette lighter. Popular options included the Special SIX or Challenger V-8; Fordomatic Drive; 4-Speed manual transmission; radio; air conditioner; Power Steering; and Deluxe or Wire Wheel Covers.

Bucket Seats were offered as an Option in the Type 62C, and the hood ornament and a special single-line side trim were available to dress up the standard Falcon 2- and 4-door Sedans.

1964 Type 62B Futura 2-door Sedan

Hood ornaments were standard on all Futura models and an Option on the Falcon Sedans hence are not reliable identification features; other frontal items are common to all.

Mr. & Mrs. George Washbun, Kailua-Kona, Hawaii

Rear windows of Sedans lower into quarters but do not retract the trim.

Bright-metal trim dresses the side windows of the Futura 2-Door. This feature is also an Option on the Falcon 2-Door.

All Futura models have its unique side trim.

Sedans have the "Thunderbird inspired" roof pillar.

All Sedans have a bright-metal serrated trim at the bottom of the roof pillar.

Lower roof pillar trim wraps around to improve appearance.

A bright-metal trim frames the rear window of the Sedans on three sides but is not used across the bottom.

Falcon rear package shelf is made of an unfinished composition board. In it, when optioned, are mounted the rear seat speakers, either conventional or Studio-Sonic.

All models display the F-A-L-C-O-N at rear; Futura has name in emblem at right of lower bright-metal trim.

Sedan dome light is courtesy-lighted in Futura Sedans, head-light-switch operated in others (unless Optioned).

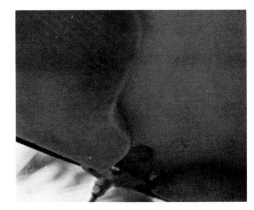

All Sedans have dual sun visors as standard equipment.

1964

Inside door handles for 1964 differ from 1963 and earlier styles (page 143).

This emblem appears on the front door panels in Futura models other than Sprint which has an interchangeable emblem of its own (page 158).

Futura Sedan rear seat is upholstered in similar fashion to Hardtop and Convertible.

Futura upholstery trim emblem appears in center panel of rear seat.

Either of the divided front bench seat backs fold to gain access to rear.

Futura Sedan has full-width dress-up trim of the Hardtops and Convertibles.

Glove box trim piece has lettered F-A-L-C-O-N and stylized insignia.

Right side corner piece is the fourth of the four pieces necessary to complete the full-width instrument panel trim set. Padded Instrument Panel above it is an Option.

With side windows lowered, Hardtop window dividers are eliminated.

Futura Hardtop is available in bench seat (Type 63B & 63E) and with bucket seats as the Futura Sports Coupe (Type 63C).

1964 Type 63B Futura 2-door Hardtop

With windows raised, the Hardtop is fully enclosed and displays window divider trim.

Ms. Pamela Goodman, El Cajon, California

Installation of a hood ornament requires two holes that are not present on non-ornament hood, but these could easily be drilled.

This is the emblem provided on fenders of V-8 equipped cars other than Sprints (page 149) which have a distinctive version.

All Futura models (other than Sprints) have a tri-color emblem on the front fenders behind the wheel well.

Tri-color Falcon emblem is distinctive Futura identification but is omitted on Sprint in favor of script emblem.

Futura door panels have bright-metal trim and deluxe type arm rests.

Emblem appears under vent window post on front door panels. A "Sprint" emblem appears in those models in its place.

Painted Futura script appears at right side of rear panel in the bright metal trim. Sprint (page 155) has its equivalent.

F-A-L-C-O-N appears on rear panel.

Other items including Taillights, gas cap, and rear bumper are the same on Sprint or Futura.

Hardtop headliner edge is concealed behind the chromed trim.

Futura Hardtops and Convertibles have chromed inside windshield moldings. In addition, the visor arms are also chromed.

Chromed center bracket supports inner ends of visors.

Hardtop chromed side piece is notched to clear trim; Convertible equivalent is not (page 180) thus the two are not interchangeable.

Futura's bench rear seat is nicely upholstered to suggest buckets, but actually seats three in comfort.

Front bucket seats are standard in the Sports Futura Hardtop; bench seats front and rear in the Hardtop.

Instrument panel is normally painted as seen here; the padded instrument panel is an available Option.

1964 FORD TRUCKS
FALCON RANCHERO-SEDAN DELIVERY

Two Sales folders were issued for the 1964 Ranchero. The mid-year version (left) dated 2/64, added a new engine Option, the 200 cubic-inch 116 horsepower SIX and a new Courtesy Light Package Option.

1964 Type 66B Ranchero with Optional

Much confusion exists regarding the 1964 Ranchero Body Side Trim. In general, it could properly be ordered as an extra-cost Option on any of the three Body Types (66A, 66B-Deluxe, or 66H-Bucket Seats), but is less likely to appear on the standard Type 66A. There is no Body Type number assigned to identify those cars on which the Option appears.

The Optional Body Side Trim is not an integral part of the Deluxe Ranchero external trim which includes only the bright-metal trim on the cab back and around the top of the cargo box, but is generally associated with it since it was rarely optioned on the standard model.

Body type 66H indicates bucket seats in place of standard bench.

1964 Type 66A Ranchero

1964 Type 66H Ranchero

Body Side Moldings

Mr. & Mrs. George Shea, Mission Viejo, California

Mr. Bill Ayers, Vista, California

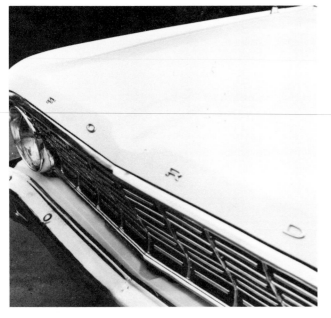

The 1964 hood interchanges with other models, but does not have the hood ornament found on Futuras.

Ranchero Gas Cap is oval-shaped, has distinctive rectangular knob, and is painted body color.

Presence of the optional 260 V-8 engine (available in all three Ranchero body Types) is indicated by this front fender ornament.

1964 Ranchero front end does not differ in appearance from the 1964 Sedans which also lack the hood ornament (Wire Wheel Covers are a dress-up Option).

Optional Body Side Trim package is same as the Futura side trim for 1964.

Chevron trim on rear fender is part of the Optional Body Side Trim package.

Type 66H Ranchero is the designation assigned for the Deluxe model with factory bucket seats. Seats were furnished both with, and without, the optional center Console.

The Ranchero spare wheel is secured vertically beneath the package shelf in a space behind the driver's seat.

Standard Ranchero, type 66A, continues to offer the "Western Motif" steerhead-pattern interior as previously. The Deluxe Ranchero, Type 66B, has red or black pleated vinyl upholstery with matching red or black steering wheel with horn ring.

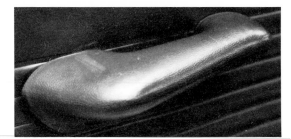

Type 66A, standard Ranchero, is supplied with plain arm rest.

Deluxe Types 66B and 66H have Futura-style door panels and larger molded Futura arm rests.

Ranchero window riser cranks have all-black knobs.

An unexplained, but fairly common, variant that seemingly serves no useful purpose is a hole which appears in both doors of some 1964 Rancheros. The panel to the right displays this plugged hole which is missing on car in photo above. Inspection of the area behind plug reveals no accessible adjustments.

The 1964 Wagon and Ranchero taillight housings differ from the similar passenger car items due to more vertical rear panel on the former. See page 245 for details.

The standard Type 66A Ranchero has an available Deluxe Interior Option, but its door panels do not include the Futura interior door panels used on Types 66B and 66H (previous page).

The Deluxe trim of the 1964 Ranchero does not include the instrument panel dress-up (page 159). Rather, the standard painted instrument panel prevails.

New body style for 1964 requires a new tailgate (compare page 136).

A red or black two-spoke steering wheel with chromed horn ring is a part of the Deluxe trim which also includes the bright-metal trim around top of box, back of cab, and side windows; cigarette lighter; dome light door switches; and red or black all-vinyl upholstery.

The optional Deluxe Trim package provides red or black vinyl bench seat upholstered in a fashion to suggest bucket seating.

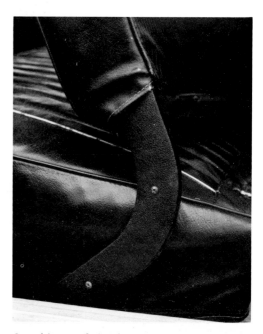

Seat hinges of the folding backs are covered with a plastic trim panel finished in a matching color.

Seat Belts are an Option for 1964.

1964

Interior air is drawn in through these screened openings inboard of the headlights.

The 1964 Club Wagon has a three-spoked black steering wheel with a distinctive chromed horn button.

Front view can easily be mistaken for the similar Econoline.

1964 Type 89B Club Wagon

The Club Wagon, Deluxe Club Wagon, and the Station Bus are three Falcons closely related to the Econoline. They were produced from 1962 on as a part of the Falcon line, but when discontinued in 1967, were joined to the Econoline line and the name Falcon dropped from the surviving models.

The principal point of identification of these Falcons (as opposed to Econolines of the same years) are, in addition to the script nameplates, the triangular-shaped windows just behind the front doors.

These Falcon models were designed as passenger-carriers, rather than cargo-carriers and used some of Falcon's trim and interior items in that effort. All were offered with standard driver's and passenger's seats flanking the engine housing, and the Club Wagon and Deluxe Club Wagon had optional second and/or third seats for up to eight passengers. All had double-door openings at rear and side and two front doors for a total of six, and a retractable step which extended when side doors were opened.

Falcon chromed script appears on both front doors and also on right rear door.

Fire Department, City of Avalon, California

The
Total Performance
1965 FALCONS

Models:

Type	54A	4-Door Sedan
	54B	Futura 4-Door Sedan (Bench)
	54D	4-Door Sedan
	59A	2-Door Station Wagon
	62A	2-Door Sedan
	62B	Futura 2-Door Sedan (Bench)
	62D	2-Door Sedan
	63B	Futura 2-Door Hardtop (Bench)
	63C	2-Door Hardtop
	63D	2-Door Hardtop (Buckets)
	66A	Standard Ranchero
	66B	Deluxe Ranchero
	66G	Standard Ranchero (Buckets)
	66H	Deluxe Ranchero (Buckets)
	71A	4-Door Station Wagon
	71B	Futura 4-Door Station Wagon
	71C	4-Door Squire
	76A	Convertible (Bench)
	76B	Convertible (Buckets)
	76D	Convertible
	78A	Standard Sedan Delivery
	89B	Club Wagon
	89D	Deluxe Club Wagon
	89C	Station Bus

Options:

Deluxe Wheel Covers (3 types)
Power Brakes
Backup Lights
Sprint Package
   includes 200 hp Challenger V-8;
   bucket seats; Sprint front fender
   emblems; console (Convertible only).
4-speed Manual Transmission
Cruise-O-Matic drive
Ford Air Conditioner
Power Steering
Seat Belts (Standard on Futura Hard-
   top & Convertible)
Electric Clock
Visibility Group
   includes remote-control outside mir-
   ror; day/night inside mirror; wind-
   shield washer and 2-speed electric
   wipers.
Padded Instrument Panel
Padded Sun Visors
AM Radio
Rear Seat Speaker
Vinyl Roof Covering (Hardtop only)

Bucket seats with or without console
Tinted Glass
White sidewall or low profile Tires
Limited Slip Differential
Emergency parking & taillight Flasher
Heater-Defroster
Courtesy Light Group
   includes ash tray; glove box; trunk;
   backup; map; and front and rear
   courtesy switches in doors.
Two-tone paint (16 choices) Sedans only
Rocker Panel Moldings
Etc.

1965 Falcons were presented in the "Total Performance" manner. With the big new 289 engine an available Option, the car was certainly well powered, but hardly then an "economy" car. The standard SIX however, had new valving which was said to increase fuel economy by up to 15%. The 200 cubic inch 120 hp Falcon Special SIX had a seven-bearing crankshaft for smoothness, but the earlier 260 V-8 was no longer offered.

A new automatic transmission, the 3-speed Cruise-O-Matic made its first appearance, and another Option, the manual 4-Speed transmission was continued.

Emphasis formerly accorded the Sprint models was reduced as "Sprint" became more obviously merely a special trim package added to otherwise-available Options of the 289 V-8 and bucket seats which could also have been ordered in the Futura Convertible or Hardtop.

1965 Falcon Specifications

COLOR AND UPHOLSTERY SELECTIONS: Pick your favorite color from 15 brilliant Diamond Lustre Enamel single tones, or 16 two-tone combinations (single tones only on convertibles and hardtops). You have a total of 31 Falcon upholstery choices of rich vinyls or combinations of cloth and vinyl. Counting standard trims and options, you have 13 choices in Falcon sedans, 12 choices in hardtops and convertibles, and 6 in wagons. (In some cases a trim is offered with more than one model.) Your Ford Dealer will be happy to show you actual samples of new Falcon colors and upholsteries.

FALCON DESIGN: The many Falcon features include: welded integral body and frame (quietness, high strength-to-weight ratio); body fully insulated and weather sealed; parallel-action electric windshield wipers; Deep-Dish steering wheel; dual sun visors with retention clips; Safety-Yoke door latches; Center-Fill fueling; counterbalanced hood and deck lid; 16-gallon fuel tank.

ENGINES: *105-hp Falcon Six* (std. all models)—170 cu. in. displ.; 3.50" bore x 2.94" stroke; 9.1 to 1 comp. ratio; reg. fuel; single-barrel carb.; auto. choke; self-adj. valves; oil cap'y, incl. filter, 4.5 qt.

120-hp Fairlane Six (opt.)—200 cu. in. displ.; 3.68" bore x 3.13" stroke; 9.2 to 1 comp. ratio; 7 main bearings. Other specifications same as standard Falcon Six.

200-hp Challenger V-8 (opt.) — 289 cu. in. displ.; 4.00" bore x 2.87" stroke; 9.3 to 1 comp. ratio; reg. fuel; 2-barrel carb.; auto. choke; self-adj. valves; oil cap'y, incl. filter, 5 qt.

ENGINE FEATURES: Falcon engine economy and durability are results of modern, efficient design, high quality materials and painstaking manufacture. Other contributing factors include: 6000-mile (or 6-month), full-flow oil filter; 36,000-mile (or 3-year) fuel filter; replaceable, dry-element air cleaner; year-round 190° thermostat; 12-volt electrical system; 38-amp. alternator; 54-plate 45 amp-hr battery; weatherproof ignition system; positive-engagement starter; new-design exhaust system with aluminized transverse muffler.

CLUTCH AND MANUAL TRANSMISSIONS: Non-centrifugal clutch with Sixes; semi-centrifugal clutch with V-8. Face diameter 8½" with Sixes, 10" with V-8.

3-Speed Transmission (std. on Sixes) has forged bronze synchronizers in 2nd and direct for smooth operation. Anti-friction bearings throughout. Standard "H" shift pattern with lever on steering column. *Synchro-Smooth Drive* (std. on V-8) has synchronized manual shifting in all three forward gears; clash-free downshifting to low while under way. *4-Speed Transmission* (opt. on V-8) with floor-mounted stick shift. All forward gears synchronized for fast, smooth shifting.

CRUISE-O-MATIC DRIVE: (opt. all engines)—Features lightweight construction with cast-aluminum converter housing. Three forward speeds, one reverse. Two selective driving ranges; 3-speed range starting in low for all normal driving, or 2-speed range for more surefooted driving on slippery surfaces. Effective engine braking in low range for better control on grades and hilly driving.

REAR AXLE: Semi-floating type with deep-offset hypoid gears. Induction-hardened, forged shafts with permanently lubricated wheel bearings.

FRONT SUSPENSION: Ball-Joint type with coil springs pivot-mounted on upper arms. 36,000-mile (or 3-year) lube intervals, full-life seals. Angle-Poised design for anti-dive control. Link-type, rubber-bushed ride stabilizer. Tapered roller wheel bearings. All-weather shock absorber fluid for better year-round ride control.

REAR SUSPENSION: Asymmetrical design with rear axle forward of spring center for anti-squat on takeoff. Long, wide-leaf springs with tip inserts and wide spring base provide soft, stable, levelized ride. Diagonally mounted shock absorbers have all-weather fluid.

STEERING: Recirculating-ball type steering gear provides easy handling. Anti-friction bearings throughout. Permanently lubricated steering linkage joints. Overall steering ratio, 27 to 1. Turning diameter, 38.8 feet. Improved power steering option with 22 to 1 ratio for faster, more responsive operation.

BRAKES: Self-adjusting, self-energizing design. Diameter 9" (Sixes), 10" (V-8). Molded linings for longer life and fade resistance. Total lining area (sq. in.) 131 (six-cylinder models), 154 (all V-8 models).

TIRES: 4-ply rated, black tubeless with Tyrex rayon cord. White sidewall tires optional. Safety-type rims. Basic sizes: Std. Six Sedans—6.00 x 13, Futura Six Hardtop and Convert. —6.50 x 13. For other models, 6.45 x 14 and 6.95 x 14 sizes are determined by choice of engine, transmission, and special equipment such as air conditioning. See your Ford Dealer for details.

DIMENSIONS AND CAPACITIES: Overall length 181.6"; height 54.5" (sedans), 53.8" (convertible), 53.2" (hardtop); width 71.6"; wheelbase 109.5"; treads 55" front, 56" rear; fuel 16 gal.; oil 4.5 qt. (Six), 5 qt. (V-8); cooling system (with heater 9.5 qt. (Six), 14.5 qt. (V-8).

1965 Type 76A Convertible

Mr. Leo Storm, Oceanside, California

1965 Type 76A Convertible

An optional Sprint Package (available on Hardtops and Convertibles) included the 200 HP Challenger V-8 engine, bucket front seats, console (on Convertible only, although it was an available added Option on the Hardtop) and special Sprint ornamentation including this unique front fender emblem.

Mr. & Mrs. Michael Jackson, Spring Valley, California

New grille emblem appears on all 1965 models.

The hood release latch is operated at lower center of grill.

Polished aluminum bezels are removed to adjust or replace lamps.

"FoMoCo" script continues on sealed beam headlights.

Full-width grill for 1965 emphasises horizontal lines to add to apparent width. Front bumper is unchanged.

Amber parking light lenses are continued.

The hood ornament appears on all but the standard Sedans and Wagons. However, it was offered as either a part of the optional Convenience Package which could be ordered on those models or as a separate Option.

Hood is unchanged from 1964.

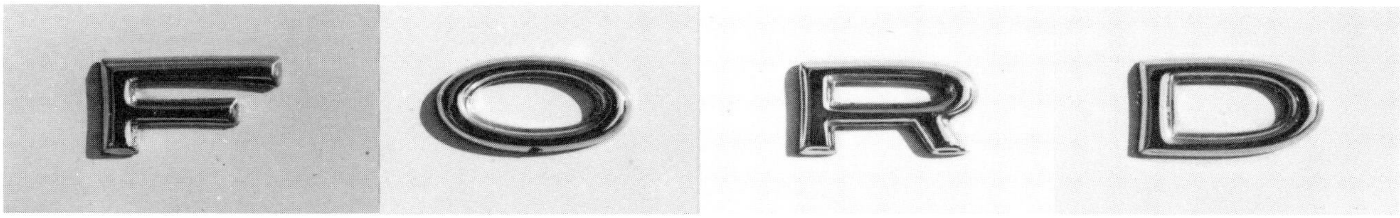

These are same letters as used on the 1964 hood.

All 1965 Futura models have this emblem on their fender flanks.

A new 289 emblem now appears for front fenders of cars with the optional V-8 engine.

Futura models have new narrower bright-metal body side trim.

Wire Wheel Covers are an extra-cost Option.

Outside door handle is unchanged from 1964.

Safety glass in side windows bears Car-Lite emblem.

Futura body side trim "breaks" around key-lock.

Body side trim has recognizable cross section.

Futura models have body side trim running length of the car.

Convertibles have handsome chromed windshield frames.

Inside ends of visor supports have rubber noise-quieting caps which are held by chromed bracket.

Sun visor brackets on Convertibles and Hardtops are chromed.

Convertible sun visors are curved and also serve as a wind deflector.

The standard floating rear-view mirror is also offered as an Optional non-glare. For 1965, the control is changed from rocker-arm (page 117) to a turn knob as seen here.

The wiper arms are unchanged.

Parallel-acting windshield wipers scrub large areas of the large windshield.

Convertibles continue to employ the clear vinyl full-width rear window.

A boot is furnished to finish off the appearance of the lowered Convertible top.

With room for six, the Convertible offers attractive transportation.

New for 1965 is this attractive gas cap used on Futura models. Falcon insignia appears in plastic center surrounded by chrome.

Gas cap is not leashed to the body and can easily be lost.

Lettering rear panel trim reads F-A-L-C-O-N. Backup lights in taillight lens are an Option.

Falcon name also appears at rear end of the Body Side Molding on Futura models only.

Luggage space in Hardtops is stated as 12.8 cubic feet, on Convertibles 9.1 cubic feet. A counterbalanced hinge holds the lid in its opened position, allowing for easy loading.

Luggage compartment has a Burtex protective mat.

The spare wheel is stored flat at the right and is held in position by a thumbscrew passing through the rectangular base of the jack.

An enlarged section at the rear of the front door sill allows for the inside door lock knob. A clear plastic grommet is used around the new chromed knob.

While 1964 and 1965 doors will interchange, the earlier door has a smaller hole and the 1965 grommet will not fit unless the hole is drilled out.

Side window glass is flat, not curved. A bright-metal frame dresses the edges of the windows on the Hardtop and Convertibles, but the Sedans lack this feature.

Date-stamping of the doorlock anvils continues.

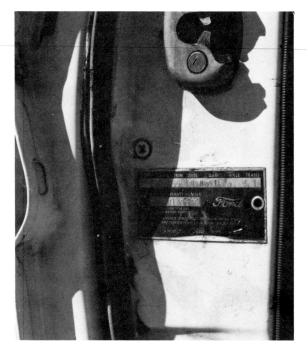

Courtesy light switches in the door posts operate the dome light in the Hardtop (map light in Convertible). These are standard in the Futura models and Optional in the Sedans.

The vehicle's data plate again appears at the rear of the left front door.

Futura door panels have a bright-metal trim strip highlighting a pleated section on which is mounted a molded arm rest and the window riser crank.

This Futura emblem appears on the inside door panels of those models. The Sprint Package substitutes a similar Sprint emblem.

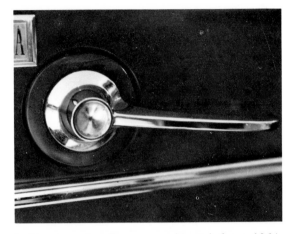

Inside door handles are unchanged from 1964. Placed behind the hub of the handle is a molded plastic spacer.

This emblem also appears on the door panels of the Futura models. To its left can be seen a portion of the bright-metal trim used on these Futura door panels.

Window riser crank handles have all-black knobs. There is no spacer used behind the hub as with the door handle (above).

Again a four-piece full-width instrument panel trim is used on the Futura models. Of plastic, chromed and painted, it dresses up the standard panel.

Turn signal knob is black, unchanged from 1964.

Although quite similar in appearance, the 1964 and 1965 steering wheels will not interchange as a change in the horn-blowing circuit results in a different hub assembly. 1964 wheel is shown above left for comparison.

Futura interiors include the chromed steering wheel horn ring as standard.

Falcon name is clearly seen at the hub of the horn ring.

1965 horn ring has patterned arms unlike 1964 style (page 160).

Black knob on transmission shift lever is similar to the turn signal knob.

The shift lever is pinned into the steering wheel collar in a rubber bushing to reduce vibration.

Optional Cruise-O-Matic automatic transmission, new for 1965, has two drive positions and provides three-speed shifting or will lock out first gear as desired. Quadrant is column-mounted above shift lever.

Standard three-speed transmission has column-mounted shift lever.

Optional padded instrument panel is provided with a bright-metal trim at its lower edge only.

The instrument cluster resembles the 1964 style (page 178) but changes in the plastic trim revise the appearance.

Futura models' instrument panel knobs are black with a chromed insert.

The vent knob beneath the instrument panel near steering column, now has plain black knob unlike the earlier style (page 158) which was lettered "A".

Parking brake handle remains unchanged.

On floor at the left is a foot-switch for depressing the headlight beam. A rubber grommet is sewn into the floor carpet to prevent fraying. Note original nylon loop carpet material.

Fuel level instrument is same as used in 1964. Only its trim is changed.

Likewise, the Temperature gauge and Turn Signal lights are changed only by appearance of the external trim.

Odometer is continued in center of instrument panel.

Under the hood, an Alternator replaces the earlier Generator calling for a revision in the trouble indicator which now reads ALT.

Low oil pressure is indicated by this OIL warning light.

The Fresh Air Heater-Defroster and also Seat Belts are installed during production on all cars; if not desired, then becomes delete Option with a blanking plate used to cover the panel cut-out.

F-A-L-C-O-N appears in black letters molded into the plastic trim panel on the glove compartment door.

A push-button latch secures the glove box door.

An optional Glove Box Door Lock offers keyed push-button.

Light and Wiper controls are to the left of the steering column.

The Optional cigarette Lighter for the Sedans comes with matching plain black knob (left) while the standard Futura cigarette lighter has a black knob with chrome insert.

Standard instrument panel has one-piece "short" plastic trim on the instrument cluster.

Balance of the instrument panel is painted.

Standard instrument panel knobs are all-black.

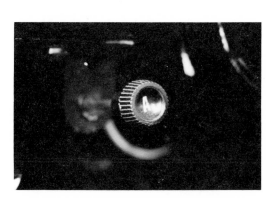

Standard models (and Wagons) "used up" many earlier items. This is the lettered air vent knob of a 1965 standard Ranchero.

Likewise, this 1964-style (note dial numbers) radio appears in the same car. Radio cut-out in panel would be covered with a blanking plate if that Option is not selected.

Replacement antenna has flat chromed escutcheon at base of mast.

Original radio antenna, right front fender mounted, has tapered chrome escutcheon at mast base.

Radio knobs will match the trim; Futura dress-up calls for black-and-chrome knobs.

New radio for 1965 displays a simplified tuning dial scale (see previous page).

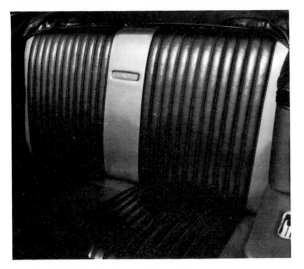

Metallic seat emblem is continued from 1964.

1965 rear seat upholstery still suggests two-passenger seating, but no longer has "bucket seat" insert used in 1964 (page 159).

Solid-color optional interior is one of six interior choices available in the Convertibles and Hardtops.

The width of the Convertible rear seat is reduced by space needed for the folding top mechanism which is concealed by formed and upholstered panels.

The rear seat ash trays in the Convertible are placed in the top surface of the end panels.

1965

The 1965 model was the last of the Falcon Convertibles. This sporty and attractive car represented the last stage of evolution for the 1966 line was to drop the model, never to be re-introduced. Superceded in both promotional effort and consumer interest by the contemporary Mustang model, the 1965 Falcon Convertible remains as a practical and highly Collectible vehicle.

A Power-operated Top is standard on all Falcon Convertibles. In 1965 it is operated by this switch on the instrument panel. The same switch is also used for the Wagon's Power Tailgate Window.

Sedans, both 2-Door and 4-Door, were produced as both "Falcon Sedans", and also as the "Futura Sedans". The Falcon Sedans were the basic models and were relatively plain. They had arm rests and ash trays in the front seats only, and little external trim. An Optionl Convenience Package was popular though and added Bright-Metal on the drip rails; a single Body Side Stripe; hood ornament; front door courtesy light switches; bright steering wheel spoke inserts; rear arm rests and ash trays; cigarette lighter; and color-keyed Floor Covering.

The Futura Sedans were more attractively trimmed, having as Standard Futura Bright-Metal Body Side Trim and hood ornament along with the side window trim. Interiors were more deluxe with ash trays and arm rests in both front and rear; cigarette lighter, etc. In addition to the power and transmission Options, color and upholstery choices were offered in Futuras that were not all available in the standard models.

1965 Type 54B Futura 4-Door Sedan

Mr. Don Rust, Carlsbad, California

Unlike Hardtops and Convertibles, the Sedans have fixed window frames that do not retract with the glass.

Rear door of 4-Door Sedan is shaped to clear the wheel well. This accounts for the need for a fixed triangular section of the glass in this door.

Sedans have traditional suspended rear view mirrors unlike Hardtops and Convertibles whose mirrors are cemented to the windshield (page 211).

Both doors of the 4-Door Sedan are hinged at the front to allow easy access for passengers on the same side.

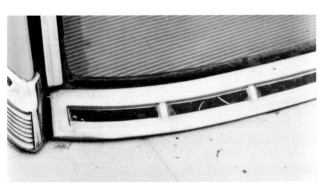

Simulated air exhausts openings are actually black-painted indents in the unique trim strip.

Sedans have bright-metal trim at base of rear roof pillar and around rear window.

Sedans all have the roofline derived from the earlier Thunderbirds.

Futura gas cap is used on Futura Sedans; a painted cap with rectangular knob appears on Falcon Sedans.

Futura Sedans have the Body Side Trim with F-A-L-C-O-N lettering on the rear fender. Standard Falcon Sedans lack this trim but have a special emblem (page 260) on their front fender flanks.

Futura Sedans have inside door panels similar to the Convertibles and Hardtops (page 216), but lack the Futura emblem that appears on them.

The 1965 molded arm rest is used on the front doors of all models.

Over-sized plastic molded spacers serve to distribute load at hub of handle.

Arm rests with integral ash trays are standard in the rear seats of Futura Sedans. They are also available as an Option in the Convenience Package, or separately, in the standard Falcon Sedans.

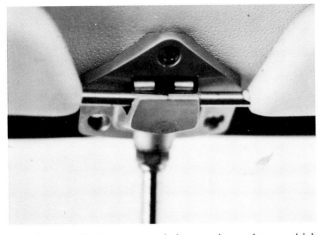

The Sedans all have suspended rear view mirrors which hang from this chromed visor support bracket at the center of the windshield molding.

Interiors in Futura Sedans continue practice of placing a bright-metal emblem at top-center of rear seats. A similar design is heat-embossed directly into the Falcon Sedan seat backs.

Futura Sedan upholstery pattern continues the suggestion of bucket seating with insert panels that extend over the top of the seat back. Futura trim emblem seen here is omitted in 2-Door version since seat back is hinged.

Bright-Metal Rocker Panel Moldings dress up the appearance of the car. These are an available Option for all models.

The 1965 Futura Sedans were said to be "the compacts most like big cars", and they were. By the standards of 1965, they were indeed compact, but in the light of the 1980's, they compare favorably in size to present production. They had standard dress-up trim including the special Futura Body Side Trim; bright-metal side window trim; a hood ornament; courtesy lighting; cigarette lighter; front and rear ash trays; etc. The result is a very attractive car that can compare favorably with presently available manufacture.

The Bright-Metal side window tirm is standard on Futura Sedans, not factory-available on the standard Falcon Sedans.

1965 Type 62B Futura 2-Door Sedan

Mr. & Mrs. Ron Evans, Vista, California

The 2-Door and 4-Door Sedans share rear window and trim.

The Falcon sedan rear package shelf is made of a composition board with a distinctive surface.

Either front seat of the 2-Door can be folded for rear compartment access. However, it is not possible to fold both seats simultaneously.

Five Futura Sedan interiors of patterned nylon cloth-and-vinyl are offered. The Falcon Sedan offers 4 cloth-and-vinyl and one all-vinyl selections.

**1965 Type 66B with Two-Tone Paint
& Ornamentation Option**

Mr. Bill Klein, San Diego, California

1965 Type 66H Deluxe Ranchero

236

Four distinct Ranchero models, Types 66A, 66B, 66G, and 66H were offered for 1965. The first two were bench seat version, Standard and Deluxe, and the second were bucket seated Standard and Deluxe models available both with and without the center console. In addition, a special Two-Tone Paint and Ornamentation Option was offered which could be applied to any of the four types. In this Option, dual Body Side Stripes (and chevron rear fender ornamentation) were furnished and the area between them painted white along with the cab roof from the belt line up. When this Option was called for on a white car, the sides and cab roof were painted red.

Standard interiors were no longer done in the familar "Western Motif" steerhead pattern, but in all-vinyl solid color with pleated inserts. At the top center of the two seat back cushion was a heat-embossed panel similar to the metal seat insert (page 225).

Standard interiors include arm rests; dome light; rear view mirror; spare tire & wheel; dual sun visors; glove box; ash tray; and a steering wheel with bright-metal horn ring. The Deluxe Trim package added bright-metal moldings around back of cab and box; Rocker Panel Moldings; added sound deadener; front floor carpeting; deluxe instrument panel; and Palomino, Blue, Black, or Red pleated vinyl seat trim with a color-keyed steering wheel; Bright-metal side and window trim; dome light door switches; and cigarette lighter.

In addition to the two six-cylinder engines and the 200 HP 2-V 289 cu. inch V-8 engine, a new Ranchero option was the 225 horsepower 4-V 289 engine, offered only with a single exhaust system.

(Bucket Seats) with Deluxe Trim Package

Mr. John Melton, Oceanside, California

Two-Tone Paint Option includes the 1964-style Body Side Trim.

White paint is confined to area within body side stripe; does not extend beyond.

Cab roof is painted from belt line up in the Two-Tone Paint Option.

Split-back bench seat folds either half for access to small rear storage compartment.

Gas cap is painted white (or red as noted) to match body side trim.

Gas caps on Standard models has rectangular knob and is painted body color.

Deluxe all-vinyl bench seat interior trim continues to suggest bucket seating by use of pleated insert panels.

The polished bright-metal body side stripe is the standard trim of the Type 66H and generally appears also on the Type 66B.

Rocker Panel Molding is included as part of the standard dress up trim of the Type 66H.

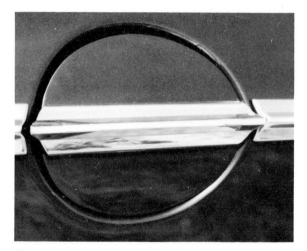

The gas cap used with the body side trim has a cast solid handle shaped and chromed to match the trim.

"Futura" metal seat upholstery trim emblems appear on the seat backs of the bucket seats.

The back of the seat backs are trimmed in a narrow vertical-striped material.

The pleated vinyl insert extends full length from the front of the bottom cushion up and over the top of the back cushion (compare the 1964 style on page 197).

1965

The traditional "receptacle" for superceded parts is the wagon/truck/Ranchero line. Here a production 1965 Type 66A Ranchero employs a 1964 door and door lock knob.

Deluxe models continue practice of using bright-metal side window trim.

Outside door handle is same as passenger cars; inside door lock knob is chromed.

The 1965 style 289 emblem appears on the front fender when that engine is optioned.

Conventional Deluxe Body Side Trim extends from front of fender insert to the taillights. Wire Wheel Covers are an Option.

Chromed Ranchero script is placed high on the fender above the body side trim.

The hood ornament is standard on the Type 66H with the exterior Deluxe Trim Package. It is also available as an Option on others.

Plastic insert of 1964-5 hood ornament is painted in five colors, Red, White, Blue, Silver, and Black.

The Ranchero hood ornament is not standard but a hood ornament is furnished with the Exterior Deluxe Trim Package, (which also includes the bright-metal Body Side Stripe and Rocker Panel Moldings).

Cab back trim of Deluxe models is brightly polished chrome. Roof drip rail moldings are bright-metal.

Lower corners are formed and chromed on Deluxe models, painted on standard.

Standard models have painted cab back and box trim. Usually painted body color, Owners frequently silver-paint to simulate deluxe chrome. Roof drip rails are painted.

The box top rails of the Deluxe models are formed of stainless steel as in the tailgate top trim. Cab back trim is cast and four chromed corners are formed and plated.

Side window frames of Standard Ranchero are painted and lack the dress up bright-metal trim.

The cab back trim of standard Ranchero is painted body color.

Trim at top of cargo box is painted on Standard Ranchero.

Lower corner pieces of trim set on Standard Ranchero are formed and painted.

This Ranchero emblem was introduced on the 1964 models and again appears on 1965 tailgate.

Block letters which spell out F-O-R-D differ from those on the hood (page 209). 7/8" high, they are same letters used on the 1962-63 hoods.

Standard taillight lens is all-red plastic with brightly chromed plastic dress up trim.

Optional back-up lights are placed in the center of the taillight lens.

Ranchero taillight lens (above left) differs from that used on other passenger car models. Note triangular section of upper vane on Ranchero lens and compare same vane of passenger car lens at the right.

Passenger car tail-
light bucket.

Ranchero/Wagon taillight bucket.

Ranchero/Wagon taillight buckets also differ from
those used on other passenger car models. Note how
Ranchero buckets (right, above) have shallower section than passenger car parts shown for comparison.

Result of incorrectly assembling a passenger car
taillight bucket in a Ranchero/Wagon is to cant
the lens upward.

Except for taillight lenses, the 1965 Ranchero rear view is
the same as that of 1964 (page 200).

1965

Loading the Ranchero over the tailgate or the sides is eased by their maximum height of only 40 inches.

With the tailgate lowered, the box floor length is almost eight feet long. Its maximum opening width of 45½ inches will almost allow flat loading of full-size plywood sheets.

The squared off rear corner's appearance is softened by a curve at the top of the box.

The tailgate structure is identical with that of the Wagons. A bright-metal trim strip at the top conceals the opening through which the rear window glass would pass.

The tailgate is locked in its upright position by latches affixed to the frame at either side.

Self-storing folding support arms are an improvement on chains offered on many other pickups.

The Falcon tailgates are spring-counterbalanced and easy to operate with only one hand.

Moving the knob to the right releases the tailgate latch. The hard rubber knob can be pressed into an opening matching its cross-section thus preventing unlatching.

Ranchero has all-steel floor, serrated both for strength and ease of moving cargo.

Nineteen of these special 5/16 NC Fillister/Phillips head screws secure the floor panel.

Flat rear window is continued. A plain rubber gasket surrounds the glass and the bright-metal (or painted) trim is on the cab back.

Access to the shock absorber upper ends is by removal of a floor panel at the forward part of the cargo box. The area beneath would otherwise be foot room in a Wagon as floor sections otherwise match.

Courtesy light door switches are placed in the door jambs of Deluxe models and operate the dome light.

1965 molded and color-keyed arm rest is used on all models.

Falcon lower door hinges have spring-operated cam to hold door in opened position; upper hinge lacks this feature.

Deluxe Ranchero employs the Futura inside door trim. Control at top right is for outside Remote Control Mirror, an available Option.

Deluxe Ranchero includes the Futura dressup trim on its instrument panel.

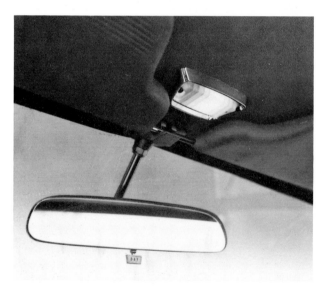

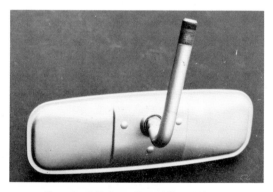

Standard Falcon Rear View Mirror.

Ranchero dome light is same light as originally used in the 1960 Sedan (page 45). Optional non-glare mirror interchanges with standard mirror and suspends from same bracket.

1965 Optional non-glare mirror is adjusted by rotating a labeled knob beneath mirror (compare page 117).

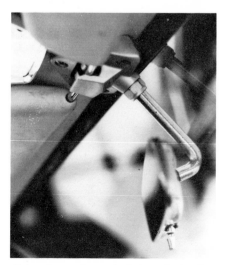

Rear view mirror shaft has distinctive shape which thrusts forward following curve of the windshield.

Optional Four-speed Manual Transmission shift knob displays shift pattern which matches that of standard size Fords.

Chromed round dressup plate secures the lower edge of a rubber boot around the shift lever of the 4-speed.

Back of seat, when adjusted fully rearward, barely clears the package shelf.

Spare wheel is secured behind driver's seat. Behind it is the jack column in brackers provided for the purpose; at the hub, is the jack base under a thumbscrew.

Squire's wood-grained side trim extends to front of fender and is framed by fibre-glass "wood" trim.

Falcon's Wagons and Club Wagons are described in special "1965 Wagons" folder which includes those in the full-size Ford and Fairlane lines.

Beginning in 1964, the Squire wood-grain side trim became solid and dark horizontal lines that previously had simulated wood strips were eliminated.

1965 Type 71C 4-Door Squire

Mounted on the front fenders, a conventional chromed Falcon script emblem is joined by a similar "Squire" piece in identifying the car.

Four Wagons were again included in the 1965 Falcon line. Of these Falcon Wagons were the least elaborate models, but even these had foam-padded seats; dual sun visors; front arm rests; front ash tray; color-keyed two-spoke deep dish steering wheel; roll-down tailgate window; electric windshield wipers; a black vinyl-rubber floor mat, and the new engine-mounted alternator. On its front fender flanks appeared the Falcon emblem (page 260), but no other ornamentation.

Very early 1965 Futura Wagons had a short body side trim extending from the front fender to the back of the front door. Those manufactured after 10/6/64 employed the full-length Futura Body Side Stripe found on the passenger cars (page 210). In addition, to the standard items above, the Futura

Wagons also featured the 120 hp Fairlane SIX engine; rear arm rests and ash trays; cigarette lighter; Color-keyed Carpeting; a Color-Keyed vinyl-rubber cargo mat; Courtesy Lighting; and a Color-Keyed 2-spoke deep-dish steering wheel with chromed Horn Ring.

The Falcon Squire included all of the above plus Simulated Wood Body Trim, Power Tailgate Window, and Nameplates (top of next page) on front fenders. However, the popular Roof Rack remained an extra-cost Option.

Despite its attractive appearance, the Falcon Squire Wagon was to be dropped from production at the end of the 1965 model year.

Mr. & Mrs. Willie West, Oceanside, California

As with the Sedans, the rear door window on the 4-Doors is divided and only the rectangular section can be lowered. Bright-metal side window trim is standard on Squire and Futura wagons.

The V-8 engine emblem apepars on the lower front fender flanks of the Squire rather than front as it does on ther models (page 209).

Passengers are able to enter both front and rear seats at the same time with forward-hinged doors.

Squire's outline wood-grain panels run full length of body sides.

Wagon rear view mirror differs from Sedans and Ranchero (pages 230 & 250). Although all are suspended, the design is not the same.

Four Bright-Metal rails are installed on the roof as part of the optional luggage rack.

Four of these stanchions support the encircling rails of the roof rack.

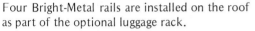

The optional Roof Rack is available for installation on any Wagon, not only the Squire.

Rear quarter glass for wagons is curved attractively.

Squire gas cap is wood-grain paneled and knob painted a matching brown. Falcon Wagons use same shape, painted caps. The Futura wagon cap is most unusual as it has two pieces of molding and a color (red, white, or black) insert to match the body side stripe.

The Power Tailgate Window is an Option on all but the Squire where it is included as standard equipment. It is operated either by a switch on the instrument panel (far left) or by an ignition key-operated switch on the tailgate.

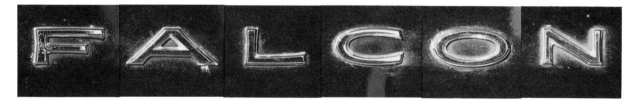

The block letters used on the tailgate are same type as used on hoods in 1964/65. ¾" high, they appear slightly compressed when compared to the tailgate letters used on Ranchero and Sedan Delivery (page 244).

With tailgate up and window extended, the Wagons are snugly sealed.

Tailgate window may be partially lowered to provide excellent air flow through the interior.

Window must be fully retracted in order to open the tailgate.

With tailgate down, cargo must be lifted only about 27" from street level into the rear cargo space.

Tailgate latch is operated by a release assembly like that of the Ranchero and Sedan Delivery. Depressing knob into shaped cut-out locks tailgate.

Cargo floor is provided with a vinyl-rubber protective mat.

Wagon second seat in normal position.

First step in folding. Folded support arm is brought up and over bottom cushion as it is rotated forward.

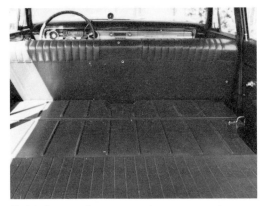

Folded second seat extends cargo area by over three feet.

With sturdy support arms touching floor, metal back of rotated seat cushion lies flat.

Result is a flat continuation of the rear cargo floor providing over nine and half feet of load length with tailgate lowered.

Seat back cushion is released and folded forward.

Squire and Futura wagons have Futura interiors. The conventional metal seat back emblem appears on the seat backs both front and rear.

Futura and Squire Wagons have rear seat arm rests which have integral ash trays.

Rear seat arm rest ash trays have hinged covers and lift out for easy emptying.

Solid rear quarter panel of Sedan Delivery provides excellent billboard space as well as protection for the interior.

Rear vision is restricted, and backing Sedan Delivery out of an angled parking space is a challenge.

The Falcon emblem appears on front fender as it does on the standard Falcon Sedans.

1965 Type 78A Standard Sedan Delivery

The Sedan Delivery was an interesting vehicle produced in the Falcon line from 1961 through 1965. Offered as a prestige vehicle for quick and light delivery loads, it provided the closed body protection missing in the similar Ranchero.

Designed to haul up to 700 pounds, it offered a unique styling and, to a degree, passenger-car-like comfort and convenience. Offered as both a Standard Type 78A and a type 78B Deluxe Sedan Delivery in 1963 and 1964, the single model listed in 1965, its final year, was the Type 78A Standard Sedan Delivery.

The Sedan Delivery was basically a 2-Door Wagon with the rear quarter windows eliminated by a solid body panel. Much of the body structure of that wagon can thus be seen in the sparse interior of the Sedan Delivery. The floor, unlike that of the similar Ranchero, is constructed of steel and weatherproof plywood with longitudinal steel skid strips.

The Sedan Delivery has 27 square feet of flat cargo floor, and 78 cubic feet of volume that is weather-protected, lockable, and accessible either from the front seat or from the lockable tailgate.

The 1965 Standard Sedan Delivery offered a Deluxe Optional Trim Package which included an arm rest on the right side door; red or black vinyl upholstery and steering wheel; bright-metal moldings on the door window frames; dome light door switches; and a cigarette lighter. Tailgate window was manually operated, but the optional Power Tailgate Window was available.

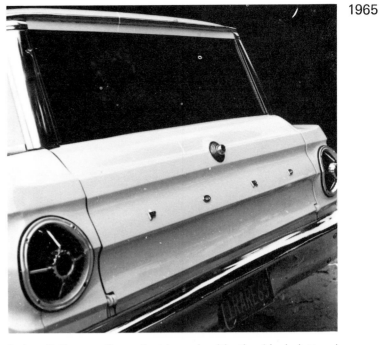

Sedan Delivery tailgate is trimmed with the block lettered F-O-R-D, not F-U-T-U-R-A as on the Wagons (page 256).

Mr. & Mrs. Mike Blodgett, Torrance, California

Block letters on front are unlike those used on other Falcons.

Large windshield gives excellent visibility to driver seated immediately behind it.

Incoming air for interior ventilation enters behind screen adjacent to the headlamps.

1965 Type 89C Falcon Station Bus

The Falcon Station Bus and Standard and Deluxe Club wagons were part of the Wagon line and continued to be offered through 1967 virtually unchanged. Their six-door accessibility (with double-doors at the curbside and rear) and a flat level floor almost nine feet from front to rear gave them a versatility unmatched.

These vehicles were built on a shortened wheelbase, only 90 inches, compared to 109.5 for the other Falcon models. Yet their interiors could accommodate almost 194 cubic feet of cargo. With an Optional heavy-duty suspension, they were rated for a one-ton payload!

The Station Bus was the basic model, and included as standard the 105 HP SIX; 3-speed transmission; 2-speed electric wipers; 3-spoke deep-dish steering wheel; adjustable driver's seat; a front passenger seat; arm rests; ash tray; dual horns; dome light; and a retractable side step that opened with the curbside door. Hub caps were painted.

The Club Wagon included all that plus a full-length color-keyed vinyl-coated rubber floor mat; full-length headlining; painted left-hand outside mirror; windshield washers; cigarette lighter; white steering wheel with chromed horn ring; dual sun visors; and bright hub caps.

The Deluxe Club Bus had padded instrument panel and sun visors; Bright left-hand outside mirror and bumpers; Bright Body Side Molding with anodized aluminum insert; and a spare tire cover.

Few changes were made in appearance through life of the production run.

Falcon Club Wagon Options
Tinted Windshield; Driver's Seat with Folding Back; All-Transistor Radio; Camper Kits including a Buffet Table, Storage Cabinet and Folding Door Shelf etc.; Cruise-O-Matic Drive; Two-Tone Paint (except Deluxe Club Wagon); White Sidewall Tires; Emergency Flasher; Second Row or Second and Third Row Seats; Pivoting Rear Door Windows; Locking Differential; etc.

Mr. Brian Templeton, Oceanside, California

Conventional Falcon chromed script appears on front and rear right-hand door.

Large front doors have vent windows that pivot open plus conventional roll-down panes.

All Falcon Club Wagons had this uniquely-shaped fixed window just behind front doors.

Curbside doors, like rear doors, are dual and when both are opened, provide an access almost four feet wide. A rectractable side step just beneath extends when door is opened.

The third of three Falcon script emblems slants upwards on right rear door.

Taillight lenses are plain and recessed; lighted license plate holder is placed on the lefthand door. Large windows provide excellent visibility.

Club Wagon's Instrument Panel is well integrated but its only similarity to that of other Falcon models is in the use of black knobs with chromed inserts.

Removable Second and/or Third Seating is an Option; normal seating is two-passenger only.

Front doors have standard arm rests in all models. black steering wheel in the Station Bus is replaced with a white wheel with horn ring in the two Club Wagons.

Falcon 1966

Models
62A Club Coupe
62B Futura Club Coupe (bench)
62C Sports Coupe (buckets)
54A Falcon 4-Door Sedan
54B Futura 4-Door Sedan
71A Falcon (4-Door) Wagon
71B Futura 4-Door Wagon
66A Standard Ranchero
66B Custom Ranchero
89B Club Wagon
89D Deluxe Club Wagon
89C Station Bus

Cover of the early-year 1966 Sales Folder (right) had a new Sports Coupe silhouetted by a stylized bird. Perhaps thought to be too ominous, it was revised in 1/66 and a scenic background stripped in.

1966 Type 62B Futura Club Cou

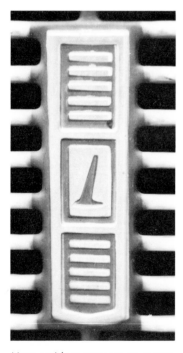

New emblem appears at center of 1966 grille. Unlike the separate 1965 emblem, this is stamped and painted directly on grille.

1966 Type 54A Falcon 4-Door Sedan

266

Mr. & Mrs. Warren Peterson, San Marino, California

Mr. & Mrs. John Higginson, Avalon, California

Options & Accessories
Power Steering; Selectaire Conditioner; Cruise-O-Matic Drive; Electric Clock; AM Radio; 120 hp Fairlane SIX or 200 hp 289 V-8 engine; Power Brakes; Visibility Group including remote-control outside mirror, day/night interior mirror, 2-speed electric wipers; Deluxe Wheel Covers; Deluxe Seat Belts with retractors and reminder light; Courtesy Light Group including lighted ash tray, glove box, trunk, map light and rear door courtesy switches; 4-Speed Manual Transmission (V-8 only); Ford Air Conditioner; WSW Tires; two-tone paint; vinyl roof on 2-Doors; roof luggage rack; Wagon Magic Doorgate; Tinted Glass all-around; Limited Slip Differential; Power Tailgate Window; and others.

Chromed Futura script appears on front fenders of those models; Falcon script appears on others.

Futura models have a bright-metal rocker panel molding and bright-metal side window trim. New curved glass appears in side windows.

Redesigned outside door handles are more angular than earlier style (page 210). Note rectangular push-button.

1966 "slab-sided" styling provides a single break line down the sides from the front to forward part of rear fender.

Cruise-O-Matic quadrant is now night-lighted along with rest of instrument panel.

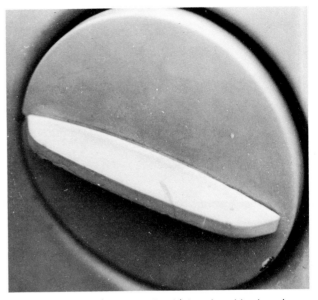

Round gas cap (with new knob) is painted body color.

Side indent runs to forward part of rear fender. Fuel filler is now on left rear fender of all models replacing center rear fill of 1965 passenger models.

Although resembling the 1965 style, taillight lenses and buckets do not interchange. Now standard, backup lights are installed in the center of the taillight lens.

Large taillights are a continuing style typical of the earlier Falcons.

Script at right rear of luggage compartment lid reads "Falcon" on all models.

1966 Ranchero front end is unmistakably typical Falcon. Re-styled block letters spell F-O-R-D on hood lip.

1966 Ranchero Sales Folder carefully omits the word "Falcon", and car is described as a "1966 Ford Ranchero".

TIRE USAGE		
MODELS	ENGINES	STANDARD TIRE 4 PLY RATING
SEDANS except Sport Coupe	6 cyl.	6.50x13
	8 cyl.	6.95x14
SPORT COUPE	All engines	6.95x14
STATION WAGONS	All engines	7.75x14
RANCHERO	All engines	7.35x14

Ranchero is listed in the tire usage table of the 1966 Falcon Owner's Manual.

The 1966 Ranchero was delivered with a conventional 1966 Falcon Owner's Manual.

1966 Type 66B Custom Ranchero

Popularity of the Ranchero (and fading popularity of the Falcon) caused Ford to withdraw the model from the Falcon line. Starting with a larger vehicle, in 1966 Ford dropped the Falcon name from the car as they phased it in to the Fairlane line. In almost all ways, Ranchero was divorced from Falcon. However, there were exceptions; the front end sheet metal and trim was clearly Falcon.

Built on a longer wheelbase (111" vs 109.5" in 1965), the 1966 Ranchero seemed "larger" as it was. Overall it had grown longer, wider, and heavier and its load-carrying capacity was now up to 1250 pounds (against 1000 in 1965).

Two models were offered. The Standard having a heater-defroster; bright horn ring; padded dash & visors; seat belts; inside rear view mirror and windshield wiper/washers; emergency flashers; cigarette lighter; dome light; and arm rests. The Custom Ranchero had these and color-keyed carpets; deluxe instrument panel trim; Deluxe door panels, and a rear vinyl-covered trim panel. Optional Visibility, Courtesy Light and Seat Packages (bucket seats with or without center console; Custom model only) were also available.

Some typical Options included the 200 cu. in. SIX, the 2-V 289 V-8, or the 4-V 289 V-8; Cruise-O-Matic or manual 4-Speed transmissions; SelectAire Conditioning; back up lights; push-button radio; tinted glass etc.

$2,249*

But you'd never guess it. Outside, Ranchero is long, clean and luxurious. Plenty of room inside, too. Swept-away dash and coved floor have that expensive-car feel. Side windows are curved. Doors are wider for easy entrance. And if you want to go all out, Ranchero offers bucket seats, console, wall-to-wall carpeting, even air conditioning.

Ranchero for '66 performs luxuriously, too. Longer, wider proportions and a new front suspension give you a soft, smooth ride. Three big engines—from the new standard 200-cu. in. Six to the exciting 289-cu. in. V-8 with four-venturi carburetor—have great get-away power. Choose automatic, 3- or 4-speed stick shift. Test-drive the hot, new Ranchero. Then check your Ford dealer's cool deal! You're ahead in a Ford all the way.

*Manufacturer's suggested retail price, delivered in Detroit. Destination charges from Detroit, local taxes and fees, and options such as white-wall tires ($32) and wheel covers ($16) are extra.

Ford Ranchero

In this rare 1966 advertisement, the reference was to the "Ford Ranchero" as "Falcon" was deleted.

General & Mrs. A. Leonard, San Marcos, California

Following general styling of the Falcon passenger cars, the
1966 Ranchero has slab sides broken only by single longitudinal crease.

Falcon's chromed Ranchero script (page 240) has been replaced
on the 1966 model by this similar emblem with grooved letters.

A new 289 emblem appears to identify those cars
having either of the two Optional V-8 engines.

Stylized revision of the earlier Ranchero Steerhead
tailgate emblem appears on the rear roof pillars.

Bright-Metal Rocker Panel Moldings are standard on the
Custom Ranchero.

A Falcon-like emblem appears at steering wheel hub.

Both Standard and Custom Ranchero models have two-spoke steering wheel with horn ring.

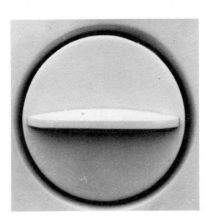

Gas cap is same as passenger car.

Taillights have round red lens; optional backup lights are placed in sector below. Top sector is decorative only.

1966 cargo box is larger, holds almost 40 cubic feet of cargo.

Restyled steerhead emblem appears on tailgate along with F-O-R-D block letters which match those on hood.

273

Better idea in economy... **Falcon '67**

Models:
Type 62A Falcon Club Coupe
      62B Futura Club Coupe (bench)
      62C Futura Sports Coupe (buckets)
      54A Falcon 5-Door Sedan
      54B Futura 4-Door Sedan
      71A Falcon 4-Door Station Wagon
      71B Futura 4-Door Station Wagon
      89B Club Wagon
      89D Deluxe Club Wagon
      89C Station Bus

A new Futura emblem now appears with Crest on roof pillar of Futura 4-Door and Club Coupe.

1967 Type 54B Futura 4-Door Sedan

Mr. Tom Colandrea, Vista, California

New grille eliminates center emblem and stresses horizontal lines.

As previously, Bright-Metal side window trim appears only on the Futura models.

Simulated side vents, appearing only for 1967, add interest to sides.

Starting in 1966, the optional radio antenna has a rectangular base.

Bright-metal side rub rail is standard on Futura models.

Taillight rims revive 1963 rings and add four quadrant stripes. Backup lights are now standard, not Options.

Fuel filler tube is routed through the luggage compartment from the left rear fender.

Rear panel trim plate has script Falcon on all models.

1967 Futura interiors offer a choice of four color-keyed nylon and vinyl and two all-vinyl solid color combinations.

A new, smaller Data Plate appeared starting in 1966, but it retained its place on the left side front door.

Bench seats are standard in the Futura Sedans and a similar divided back seat is used in the Club Coupe. Bucket seats are available only in the upgraded Futura Sports Coupe in which they are standard along with a vinyl roof trim, power front disc brakes, and one of the two V-8 engines.

New stylized crest replaces former Falcon emblem on steering wheel hub.

Day/Night inside mirror features a Shatter-Resistant, Flexible-backed Glass and breakaway or double-pivot support.

New Impact-Absorbing Steering Wheel has deep-padded hub. Horn Ring is standard on Futura models. Turn signal Lane-change feature is new this year.

Futura instrument panel has full-width plastic trim. Radio is an Option.

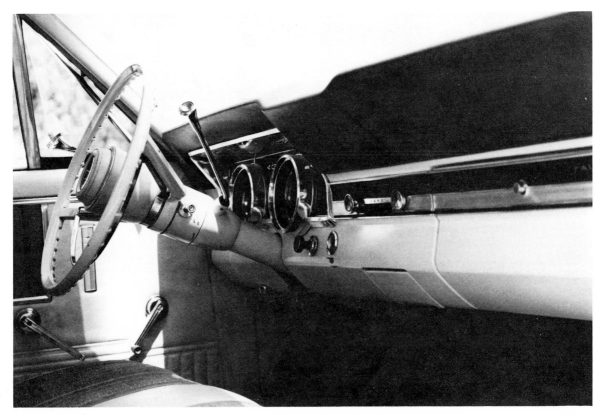

Instrument panel padding is standard on all models. Note foot-operated parking brake, first used in 1966 models.

1967 Type 71B Falcon Futura Wagon   *Mr. Clark Crouse, Encinitas, California*

A new smaller (page 272) 289 emblem appeared for 1967; note Falcon emblem on front of Body Side Trim.

Again in 1967, only two Wagons appeared in the Falcon line. The 4-Door Falcon Wagon was "standard", and the upgraded Futura Wagon comprised the whole line, the Squire having been dropped along with the 2-Door Wagons at the start of 1966.

Simulated side vents, a 1967 styling feature, appear on the fender flanks.

New Futura chromed script, appears on rear fenders of those models.

The new Falcon chromed script appears on all tailgates and on rear fenders of the Falcon Wagons.

Standard tailgate window manual crank; Power Tailgate Window was an Option.

Falcon's "Magic Doorgate", first available in 1966, allows tailgate to be lowered or opened like a door for easier entry; it became a popular Wagon Option.

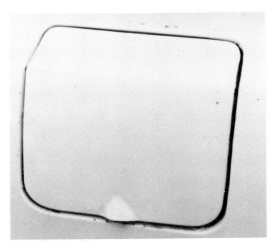

Unlike Sedans, the Wagons had an enclosed fuel cap and this access flap on the left rear fender.

No longer a part of the Falcon line, the new Fairlane Ranchero continued to be a popular model. Three styles were offered, the basic Fairlane Ranchero, the Fairlane 500, and the top-of-the-line Fairlane 500 XL which included standard bucket seats and a center console together with some special trim items.

With its transfer into the Fairlane line, new and larger engines became available and for 1967, in addition to the standard 120 hp 200 cu. in SIX, options included both a 2-V 289 V-8 and 390 V-8 and also a 4V 390 V-8 rated at 315 horsepower!

1967 is the only year that Ranchero displayed these vertically stacked headlamps.

1967 Type 66B Fairlane 500 Ranchero   *Mr. Frank Ribeiro, San Diego, California*

1967 Type 66A Fairlane Ranchero

Mr. Bob Smith, Escondido, California

The Standard Fairlane Ranchero had a relatively plain interior; but had attractively designed instrument cluster found in upgraded models.

"Fairlane" now appears in side stripe of all Rancheros; either the Fairlane seen here or the lower and wider stripe of the Fairlane 500 and the Fairlane 500/XL.

Roof pillars of Fairlane Ranchero are bare; Steerhead emblem (facing page) appeared on Fairlane 500 and XL models.

Standard backup lights are now placed in rectangular center lens and upper and lower red lenses act as taillights and directional turn signals. Very early 1967 Rancheros were equipped with 1966 style lamps.

Steerhead emblem appears on all tailgates.

Ranchero is now well identified as a Fairlane with this emblem on tailgate.

1968 FALCON...
Another better idea from FORD

Models
Type 62A Falcon Club Coupe
     62B Futura Club Coupe (bench)
     62C Futura Sports Coupe (buckets)
     54A Falcon 4-Door Sedan
     54B Futura 4-Door Sedan
     71A Falcon 4-Door Wagon
     71B Futura 4-Door Wagon

1968 was little changed from 1967. A new grille treatment revised frontal appearance, but body styles were unchanged from the previous year. Big news was the addition of the 4-V 302 cu. in. V-8 engine rated at 230 horsepower, as an available Option in Ford's Economy Car.

1968 Type 62A Club Coupe

Mr. Bud Dalton, Oceanside, California

1968 styling eliminates the simulated vents on the fenders which appeared only in 1967.

This is a reflective side marker used only on 1968 models.

Taillights assume a more rectangular shape; standard backup light again appears at its center.

The script Falcon appears on the rear fenders of those models; replaced as applicable by a script Futura. A second reflective side marker appears on rear fender.

No identification appears on Falcon Club Coupe rear deck lid. With Futura script on the sides, those models place their Falcon script on rear panel.

Four headlamps set in dual pairs are identification feature of the 1968-69 Ranchero.

The 1968 and 1969 Ranchero continued on the Fairlane/Torino chassis as larger cars capable of handling up to 1250 pounds of cargo. Interestingly, the name Fairlane was not dropped, and the three vehicles became the Ranchero, the Ranchero 500, and the Ranchero GT. In general, they followed last years concept of a basic model, an upgrade, and a top-of-the-line bucket-seated vehicle with special wheels and GT trim.

The big Ford 390 V-8 became an available Option, in two versions. With the 4-V 390, V-8 Ranchero had an available 335 horsepower.

Little change occurred in 1969 to distinguish it from 1968; side molding cross-section was revised, and a few trim pieces changed, but the car was essentially unchanged.

Highly stylized steerhead appears on rear roof pillars.

1969 Type 66B Ranchero 500

Mr. Tom Clements, Avalon, California

1968 side stripe exhibited four parallel stripes.

1969 side markers were reflective. In 1969, these became illuminated lamps at the rear.

The same taillight was used in both 1968 & 1969 Ranchero.

Round, painted gas cap is standard on all models.

Parking lights are placed outside headlamps on the fender crease, thus also serve as marker lights.

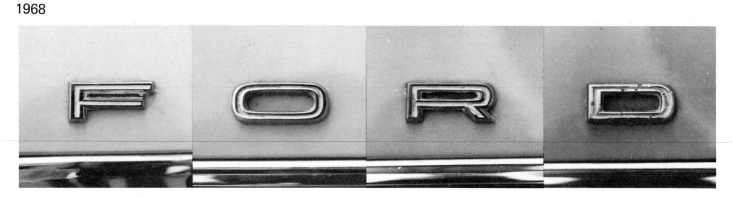

These ½ inch high letters, a new style for 1968, appear on the Ranchero hood lip in 1968-69.

Tailgate has no steerhead emblem.

Rear corner pieces emphasize length of sides while joining smoothly with tailgate trim.

In a different style, these ¾'' high letters appear on the tailgate.

Temperature, fuel level, and directional signal appear in far left pod.

Far right pod displays Alternator and Oil Pressure Warnings and directional signal.

Left center pod is speedometer with integral odometer.

Right center pod is for Optional Electric Clock.

Optional AM-FM stereo radio is integrated into the instrument panel.

New four-pod Safety-Padded Instrument Panel is nicely framed by two-spoke steering wheel with chromed horn ring (supplied in Ranchero 500 and Ranchero GT).

Models
Type 62A Falcon Club Coupe
62B Futura Club Coupe (bench)
62C Futura Sports Coupe (buckets)
54A Falcon 4-Door Sedan
54B Futura 4-Door Sedan
71A 4-Door Wagon
71B Futura 4-Door Wagon

Falcon's youthful image had just about disappeared by 1969. Even the Sales Folder, despite featuring a very young girl on the cover, introduced some fairly mature models to display the 1969 line! With no changes in the lineup, there were three Falcon models and four Futura variants for a total of seven unchanged choices. "Keyless" ignition locks which accepted reversible keys were one small new feature.

Falcon script appears on rear fender flanks of those models, rear panel of all.

A reminder of Falcon's past is this drug store display sign.

1969 Type 62A Falcon Club Coupe

Mrs. Martha Herzer, Encinitas, California

Both front and rear windows of the Club Coupes lower for ventilation.

Curved side glass, although first used in 1966 models, continues to be a featured item.

Taillight is unchanged from 1968 (page 283).

Falcon models have script word on fender flanks and on rear deck lid. The Futura script replaces the fender scripts on those models. A Local Dealer has added his script to lid.

falcon '70

Body Types
62A Falcon Club Coupe
62B Futura Club Coupe
54A Falcon 4-Door Sedan
54B Futura 4-Door Sedan
71A 4-Door Wagon
71B Futura 4-Door Wagon

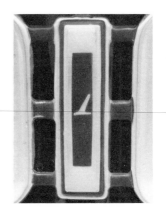

Nearing the end of its line, the 1970 Falcon saw its one "sporty" model dropped as the Futura Sports Coupe with its bucket seats and smart trim was eliminated. Only six models were offered, and but one engine Option, the 2-V 302 cu. in. V-8.

The radiator grille from 1968-70 was unchanged. This stamped and painted emblem appeared at its center.

1970 Type 62B Futura Club Coupe

Trim pieces around the windshield are the same from 1966-70.

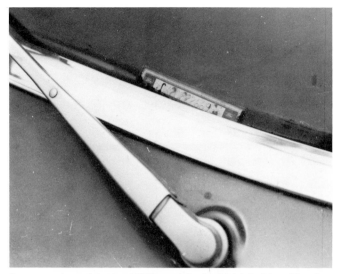

Commencing with the 1970 model, the Vehicle Identification Number appears on top of the instrument panel where it can be read from outside the car.

This Futura script emblem was introduced in 1968 and continues through 1970 model. (1967 style page 274).

Futura script again appears on the fender flanks of those models. Wheel lip molding is standard on Futura, not supplied on the Falcon models.

Rocker panel moldings are standard on Futura models. Remote-control Rear View Mirror is an Option.

Futura identification is added together with a full-width trim strip on the rear deck lid of those models.

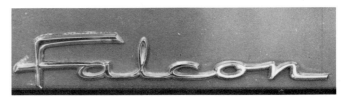

The 1968-70 Falcon script (see page 279 for comparison) is placed on the rear deck lid of all models.

Full-width bright-metal trim is Futura standard trim not supplied on Falcon Sedan or Club Coupe.

falcon '70½

FORD'S ALL-NEW
EDITION OF
AMERICA'S ALL-TIME ECONOMY CHAMP

Models
Type 62A 2-Door Sedan
     54A 4-Door Sedan
     71D Falcon 4-Door Station Wagon

On January 1, 1970, production of the "true" Falcon ended and for a short time the name was continued on Torino-based cars that received little acclaim, thus were discontinued before the end of the model year.

Larger, heavier, less attractive to many, these "Falcons" were offered with most of the Torino Options including a choice of any of seven engines ranging from the standard 250 cu. in. SIX up to a remarkable 370 horsepower 429 cu. in. 4V Cobra Jet Ram Air V-8.

Wheelbase of these cars was 117" for the Sedans which had an overall length of over 206 inches. Compared to the "compact" wheelbase of 109.5" and overall length of 181" of their progenitors in 1960, these vehicles were true behemoths! Public acceptance was limited, despite such standard features as a dual hydraulic brake system; windshield washers; backup lights; outside rear view mirror; locking steering column; etc.

The 1970½ Falcon was an extremely low production car. Due to its rather limited appeal, an unconfirmed story has it that Ford supplied its Dealers with a "Kit" which included necessary "Torino" script emblems for the rear fenders and existing cars were converted for better sales opportunities.

1970½ Type 62A Falcon 2-Door Sedan

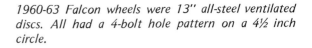

1960-63 Falcon wheels were 13'' all-steel ventilated discs. All had a 4-bolt hole pattern on a 4½ inch circle.

1960 9'' standard Hub Cap (black lettered).

1960 Optional 13'' Deluxe Wheel Cover (black depressions). 1961 same but white depressions.

1961 9'' standard Hub Cap (white lettered).

The 1962 standard Hub Cap was the same as 1960 (black lettered).

1962 Optional 13'' Deluxe Wheel Cover.

1961-62 13'' Futura Wheelcover.

Mid-1962, new 13″ Futura Wheel Cover.

1963 Optional 13″ Deluxe Wheel Cover.

1963 Optional 13″ Wire Wheel Cover.

13″ "wires" have hole in one spoke for protruding valve stem.

1963 9″ standard Hub Cap (also used in 1964) (black letters).

1963 13″ Futura Wheel Covers.

1964-up standard Hub Cap (one of three).

1964 Optional Deluxe 13″ Wheel Cover.

1964 Optional 13″ Wire Wheel Cover.

In mid-April of 1964, new 14″ diameter, 5-bolt wheels were introduced in production replacing the former 13″ wheels, but wheels on six cylinder cars continued the 4-bolt hole pattern.

1965-up standard Hub Cap (one of three in 1965).

1965 Optional 14″ Deluxe Wheel Cover (also available in 13″)

1965 Optional 14″ Deluxe Wheel Cover (also available in 13″).

Falcon emblem in red center.

14″ Wire Wheel Covers have no hole for valve stem in spokes.

1965 Optional 14″ Wire Wheel Cover.

Crest in red center of spinner.

Available in 1965 as Mustang Options, these 14″ Styled Steel Wheels also appeared on the 1966 Ranchero with distinctive red 2½″ hub caps (above).

WHEELS & WHEELCOVERS

1965-66 standard 9″ Hub Cap.

1966 Optional 13″ & 14″ Deluxe Wheel Cover with Spinner (carried over from 1965).

1966 standard 9½″ Hub Cap.

1966 Optional 13″ & 14″ Deluxe Wheel Cover (carried over from 1965).

1966 Optional 14″ Wire Wheel Cover (carried over from 1965).

1967 Ranchero Optional 14" Deluxe Wheel Cover.

During 1966, the 13" wheels used on the 6-cylinder cars were phased out and by 1967, all models rode on 14" wheels.

1966-68 Optional 14" Deluxe "Mag" Wheel Cover.

1967 Optional 14" Deluxe Wheel Cover.

1967-68 Standard 9 5/8" Hub Cap.

1968 Optional 14" Deluxe Wheel Cover.

1969-70 Standard 10½" Hub Cap.

Black center Crest.

1969-70 Optional 14" Deluxe Wheel Cover.

Are you promoting FALCON ACCESSORIES for RANCHERO PICKUPS?

1960-62 Backup Lamp installs on rear panel.

Aftermarket Rain Deflector

Aftermarket Wind Deflector

Locking gas cap, 1960 on.

1963 backup light installs in tail-light lens.

1963 Electric Clock

1963 Clock requires hole in Instrument Panel.

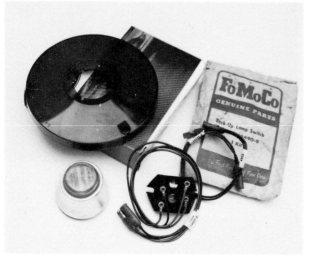

1963 Backup Light Kit

1964-65 Electric Clock

Fibre-glass Ranchero Camper Shells were manufactured by at least two Aftermarket suppliers, Dingman (upper photos), and Protect-O-Top. At recent date, Dingman was apparently out of business, but Protect-O-Top still had their shells available.

Dingman's shell provided several additional inches of headroom by raising the roof above the cab.

Dingman's additional height is apparent in this view.

A locking exterior tailgate handle was furnished on both models.

Side windows of both slide open for ventilation.

Protect-O-Top roof height matches that of cab.

Dingman and Protect-O-Top also both offered aftermarket Ranchero fibre-glass tonneau covers. Similar in concept and appearance, the Dingman product may have been a bit more sturdy.

Underside of cover displays reinforcing frame.

Dingman product has molded longitudinal reinforcing.

Top of Protect-O-Top product is flat with no bracing. Keyed latch at rear is common to both products.

Either unit offers excellent interior access.

Aftermarket tie-down rail can be installed on cover.

Several types of After-market Tie-Downs are available.

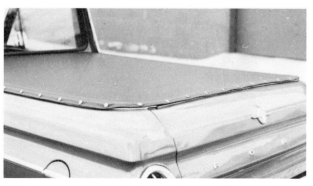

Trim shop accessory vinyl cover is secured by snap fasteners.

Convertible Consoles differ in height from those in Hardtops but the rear lower edge of all are shaped to match driveline tunnel.

Consoles were initially made of aluminum; later die cast, but appearance remained the same.

Side panels for 1962 were Red or Black; 1963 added Blue, Turquoise, and Gold.

1964-65 Console was redesigned and is less elaborate. Bright-Metal lid trim (upper left) is often missing on surviving units.

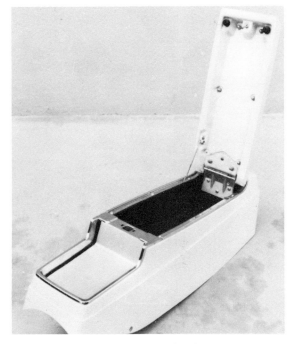

Console provides handy additional storage area between seats.

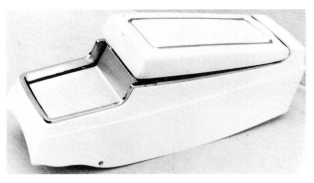

This Console was an available Option on the six-cylinder Futura Hardtop and six-cylinder Futura Convertibles in 1965. Only its lid differs from the 1964-65 Console (left).

Optional Windshield Wiper pump is foot-operated.

Optional Seat Belt Warning placed sensor under front seat upholstery and light on instrument Panel.

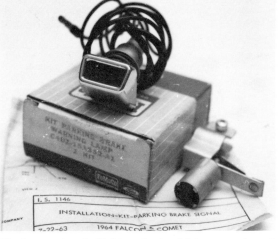

Similar optional Parking Brake Light sensed position of brake handle.

1964 optional Backup Lights replaced standard lens (right) with center-mounted lights in taillight.

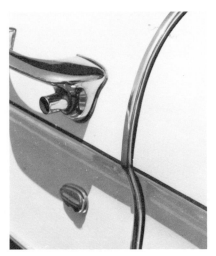

Door Edge Guards helped prevent chipping of paint.

1965 optional Backup Light lens assembly was similar but based on new taillight lens.

Falcon's transmission shift quadrant was not lighted making night driving a bit awkward. An optional quadrant light was available but not generally ordered. The standard shift lever collar was replaced with one having accommodations for a light bulb which was concealed by a shaped cap. The flat end of the cap had a lens with enscribing circle which identified the lever position.

The optional Ford AirConditioner was suspended beneath the center of the Instrument Panel.

Factory Ford AirConditioner 1964-65.

Although not available from the factory with 4-speed transmission due to initial shift lever interference, some Dealers installed the units by recessing them with special brackets.

Accessory fender-mounted lights were offered to relay turn-signal operating informaiton to the driver.

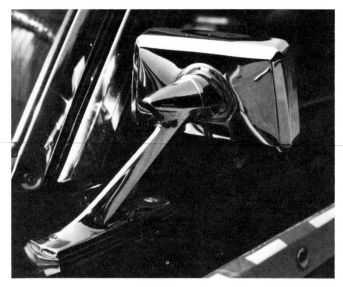

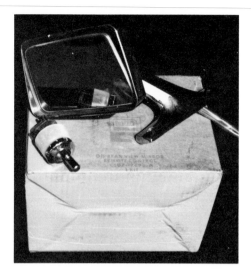

Rectangular mirror, available in both fixed and also remote-operated. Matching righthand mirror also available. 1963 up.

Chromed control knob for remote mirror is mounted on door sill.

Fairlane version has Crest.

Round remote control mirror, generally used on Mustang, was also offered on Falcons 1964 up.

Plain round mirror, 1962 on.

Falcon insignia round mirror 1963 on.

Round mirror; tapered edge, 1960 up.

Round mirror; annular groove, 1963 up.

Outside rear view mirrors prior to 1966 were Dealer-added accessories. With each Dealer's inventory of Ford (and aftermarket) parts different, there can be no consistent identification as to what might have appeared on a particular car at the time that it was delivered. This section is intended therefore only to identify some of those Ford mirrors as they appear in the Parts books.

Forward-thrusting mirror mount 1961-62.

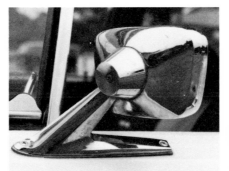

Optional 1967-70 Remote-operating; rectangular. Note difference from pre-ceeding page.

Inside Control Knob and Stand.

Map light. Also appears as standard lamp in Convertible where it functions in place of a Dome Light.

Remote Trunk Release employs Bouden Cable mechanically to release rear deck lid latch. 1965

Not an "accessory", but an interesting item, a die cast toy Ranchero by Hubley.

Carefully detailed plastic Promotional Model of 1964 Convertible, available from Dealers at introduction.

Factory air conditioning was first offered in 1961 as the PolarAire Conditioner, suspended beneath the instrument panel. In 1963 this more attractive Ford Air Conditioner appeared. Initially unavailable with the 4-speed transmission due to interference with the shift lever, the restriction was lifted late in 1965 with a mounting bracket redesign providing clearance.

Optional Rear Seat Radio Speaker, or the Studio-Sonic Reverberation unit were mounted in the rear package shelf beneath a grille.

The optional rear seat ash tray recessed into the back of the front seat of 4-Door Sedans.

Dealer-installed accessory trailer hitch was popular especially on the Ranchero.

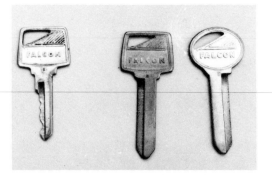

Distinctive Falcon keys 1960-66 (left) and 1967 up reversible keys.

Autolite spark plugs and pressure Radiator Cap (12-14 psi) are original equipment.

1960 Engine compartment. Note fore & aft installation of battery which was rotated to side-to-side installation in 1963 models.

1960 90 HP Falcon SIX — 144 cu. in. displacement; 3.50:: bore x 2.50" stroke; 8.7:1 compression ratio; regular fuel; manual choke; vacuum spark advance; 4-bearing crankshaft; rotor-type oil pump.

1961 85 HP Falcon SIX
144 cu. in. displacement; 3.50" bore x
2.50" stroke; 8.7:1 comp. ratio; regular
fuel; manual choke

1961 101 HP Falcon SIX
170 cu. in. displacement; 3.50" x 2.94" stroke; 8.7:1 comp.
ratio; regular fuel; manual choke

FALCON DATA PLATE ENGINE DESIGNATIONS

Cyl	V	CID	HP	1960	1961	1962	1963	1964	1965	1966	1967	1968	1969	1970
SIX	1	144	85	S	S	S	S	S						
SIX	1	170	101		U	U	U	U	U	U	U	U	U	
SIX	1	200	116					T*	T	T	T	T	T	T
V8	2	260	164				F	F**						
V8	2	289	200						C	C	C	C		
V8	4	289	225						D***	D***	D			
V8	2	302	230									F	F	F

Wagon/Ranchero Option only
** *Also available with optional Sprint dress-up kit*
*** *Wagon/Ranchero Option only*

		1970½		
SIX	1	250	155	L
V8	2	302	220	F
V8	2	351	350	H
V8	4	351	300	M
V8	4	429	360	N
V8	4	429	370 (Cobra)	J
V8	4	429	370	C
			(Cobra Ram Air)	

1963 101 HP Falcon SIX
170 cu. in. displacement; 3.50" bore by 2.87" stroke; other items same as 85 HP SIX.

1963 85 HP Falcon SIX
144 cu. in. displacement; 3.50" bore x 2.50" stroke; 8.7:1 comp. ratio; regular fuel; manual choke; single exhaust.

1963 164 HP Challenger 260 V-8
260 cu. in. displacement; 3.80" bore by 2.87" stroke; 8.7:1 comp. ratio; regular fuel; 2-barrel carburetor; automatic choke; single exhaust.

1963 164 HP Sprint 260 V-8
Same as Challenger 260 V-8 plus special trim items; power-toned air cleaner, and muffler.

Sprint 260 V-8 engine has chromed air cleaner and valve covers.

314

Courtesy Jim Osborn Reproductions, Atlanta, Georgia

Representative display of Falcon engine compartment decals.

POWER TEAMS

ENGINE	CU. IN. DISPL.	HP @ RPM	MAX. TORQUE @ RPM	BORE/ STROKE	COMP. RATIO (to 1)	CARB. & FUEL	TRANS- MISSION OPTIONS	AVAILABLE WITH MODELS
Falcon Six	144	85 @ 4200	134 @ 2000	3.50 x 2.50	8.7	1 bbl. Reg.	A-B-D	Std: All except Futura Convertibles, Sprints
Falcon 170 Special Six	170	101 @ 4400	156 @ 2400	3.50 x 2.94	8.7	1 bbl. Reg.	A-B-D	Std. Futura Convertibles, Opt. Others exc. Sprints
Challenger 260 V-8	260	164 @ 4400	258 @ 2200	3.80 x 2.87	8.7	2 bbl. Reg.	A-B-C	Opt. All Models except Sprints
Sprint 260 V-8	260	164 @ 4400	258 @ 2200	3.80 x 2.87	8.7	2 bbl. Reg.	A-B-C	Std. on Sprints

1963 Falcon offered up to a dozen engine/transmission combinations.

	SIX	V-8
Front Sway Bar	7/8"	7/8"
Drag Link	15/16"	1-1/32"
Pitman Arm	¾ x 31/32	7/8 x 1-1/16
Coil Springs	¾	13/16
Radiator inlet	1½	1-7/8
Radiator dimensions:		
Height	20½	21
Width	17½	17½
Thickness	1-5/8	2"
Exhaust pipe	1-13/16	2"

Falcons built with the V-8 engine have some heavier components. Some of these are compared in the chart above.

DECODING YOUR DATA PLATE

Owners will find interesting information appearing on the data plates of their vehicles. Such items as original color, engine, transmission type, trim (consult your local Ford Dealer), etc., can be obtained from these data plates.

1960-63 Falcon had Serial Number stamped into the left cowl to side deflector support where it can be seen when hood is raised.

TRANSMISSION CODES

Code	Type
1	3-Speed Manual
3	Fordomatic
4	Cruise-O-Matic
5	4-Speed Manual

DATE CODES

A number signifying the date precedes the month code letter. A second-year code letter will be used if the model exceeds exceeds 12 months.

Month	Code First Year	Code Second Year
January	A	N
February	B	P
March	C	Q
April	D	R
May	E	S
June	F	T
July	G	U
August	H	V
September	J	W
October	K	X
November	L	Y
December	M	Z

DISTRICT CODES (DSO)

Units built on a Domestic Special Order, Foreign Special Order, or other special orders will have the complete order number in this space. Also to appear in this space is the two-digit code number of the District which ordered the unit. If the unit is a regular production unit, only the District code number will appear.

Code	District	Code	District
11	Boston	45	Davenport
12	Buffalo	51	Denver
13	New York	52	Des Moines
14	Pittsburgh	53	Kansas City
15	Newark	54	Omaha
21	Atlanta	55	St. Louis
22	Charlotte	61	Dallas
23	Philadelphia	62	Houston
24	Jacksonville	63	Memphis
25	Richmond	64	New Orleans
26	Washington	65	Oklahoma City
31	Cincinnati	71	Los Angeles
32	Cleveland	72	San Jose
33	Detroit	73	Salt Lake City
34	Indianapolis	74	Seattle
35	Lansing	81	Ford of Canada
36	Louisville	83	Government
41	Chicago	84	Home Office Reserve
42	Fargo	85	American Red Cross
43	Rockford	89	Transportation Services
44	Twin Cities	90-99	Export

1964-65 models have serial Number stamped into left frame top with fender recessed to allow clear view.

CONSECUTIVE UNIT NUMBER

Each model year, *each* assembly plant begins production with the number 100001, and continues on for each unit built. Since not only Falcons but frequently also Mustangs and Fairlanes were built on the same assembly lines, the Consecutive Number will include these other models.

DECODING YOUR DATA PLATE

ENGINE CODE see page 313

Data Plate diagram:

```
MODEL                CONSECUTIVE                          AXLE
YEAR     MODEL       UNIT NUMBER                          RATIO

SERIAL NUMBER     MADE IN   Ford    REG. U.S.
1H12S 100001      U.S.A. BY         PAT. OFF.

BODY COLOR TRIM DATE TRANS. AXLE
 58A   M    12   20K    1      3

THIS VEHICLE IS CONSTRUCTED UNDER UNITED STATES LETTER PATENTS

2590719   2617681   2631694   2677572   2677574   2683578
2698012   1726894   2782722   2784363   2789611   2810447

          OTHER PATENTS PENDING

ASSEMBLY         ENGINE              TRANSMISSION
PLANT
```

EXAMPLE 1H12S 109299
- 1   1961 Model
- H   Lorain Assembled
- 12 4-Door Sedan
- S   6-cylinder 144 cu. in. engine

ASSEMBLY PLANT CODES

Code Letter	Assembly Plant	Code Letter	Assembly Plant
A	Atlanta	N	Norfolk
D	Dallas	P	Twin Cities
E	Mahwah	R	San Jose
F	Dearborn	S	Pilot Plant
G	Chicago	T	Metuchen
H	Lorain	U	Louisville
J	Los Angeles	W	Wayne
K	Kansas City	Y	Wixom
.	Michigan Truck	Z	St. Louis

REAR AXLE RATIO CODES

A number designates a conventional axle, while a letter designates an Equa-Lock differential.

Code	Ratio	Code	Ratio
1	3.00:1	A	3.00:1
3	3.20:1	C	3.20:1
4	3.25:1	D	3.25:1
5	3.50:1	E	3.50:1
6	2.80:1	F	2.80:1
7	3.80:1	G	3.80:1
8	3.89:1	H	3.89:1
9	4.11:1	I	4.11:1

EXTERIOR COLOR CODE

	1960	1961	1962	1963	1964	1965
A	Raven Black	Raven Black	Raven Black	Raven Black	Raven Black	Raven Black
B					Pagoda Green	Pagoda Green
C		Aquamarine				Honey Gold
D		Starlight Blue	Ming Green	Ming Green	Dynasty Green	Dynasty Green
E	Belmont Blue	Laurel Green	Viking Blue	Viking Blue		
F	Skymist Blue		Baffin Blue		Guardsman Blue	
G			Silver Mink			
H		Chesapeake Blue	Oxford Blue	Oxford Blue	Caspian Blue	Caspian Blue
I				Champagne Beige		Champagne Beige
J	Monte Carlo Red	Monte Carlo Red	Rangoon Red	Rangoon Red	Rangoon Red	Rangoon Red
K	Sultana Turquoise	Algiers Bronze	Chalfonte Blue		Silversmoke Gray	Silversmoke Gray
L			Sahara Rose			
M	Corinthian White	Corinthian White	Corinthian White	Corinthian White	Wimbleton White	Wimbleton White
N			Diamond Blue			
O						Tropical Turquoise
P			Silver Moss	Silver Moss	Prarie Bronze	Prarie Bronze
Q		Silver Gray	Silver Gray			
R		Cambridge Blue	Tucson Yellow			Ivy Green
S		Mint Green			Cascade Green	
T	Meadowvale Green		Sandshell Beige	Sandshell Beige		
U			Deep Sea Blue			
V			Chestnut		Sunlight Yellow	Sunlight Yellow
W	Adriatic Green	Garden Turquoise				
X			Heritage Burgundy	Heritage Burgundy	Vintage Burgundy	Vintage Burgundy
Y				Glacier Blue	Skylight Blue	Silver Blue
Z	Platinum		Fieldstone Tan		Chantilly Beige	
3					Poppy Red	Poppy Red

Typical Options Expressed as a Percentage of Total Production						
	1960	1961	1962	1963	1964	1965
SIX Cylinder	100	100	100	87.5	78.7	81.7
V-8 Engines	N/A	N/A	N/A	12.5	21.3	18.3
Automatic Transmission	44.5	49.0	51.6	50.5	53.2	57.3
4-Speed Manual Transmission	N/A	N/A	0.6	8.0	6.5	2.4
AM Radio	47.3	46.7	49.8	51.4	48.0	54.6
Heater	88.2	91.3	95.0	94.3	94.3	94.2
Air Conditioning	N/A	N/A	0.7	1.7	2.7	3.3
Tinted Glass						
Windshield only	N/F	6.1	15.9	21.4	18.7	18.1
All Around	N/A	N/A	2.5	1.9	1.4	2.3
Limited Slip Differential	N/A	N/A	N/A	N/A	N/A	1.2
Deluxe Wheel Covers	N/F	N/F	15.3	47.1	26.9	30.0
White Sidewall Tires	37.6	38.7	43.5	50.5	50.5	N/F
Windshield Washer	15.0	14.3	16.3	24.0	24.7	27.8
Bucket Seats	N/A	9.1	13.0	14.5	8.0	2.0

N/A Not Available

N/F No records available

From Ford Motor Company Production Records

	1960	1961	1962	1963	1964	1965
Total Units Produced	435,676	489,323	414,282	345,972	317,400	227,362
Squire Wagon	N/A	N/A	22,583	6,808	6,766	6,703
Same-Bucket Seats	N/A	N/A	N/A	1,461	N/A	N/A
Sprint Convertible	N/A	N/A	N/A	4,602	3,652	300
(Other) Convertibles	N/A	N/A	N/A	31,192	16,200	6,315
Sprint Hardtop	N/A	N/A	N/A	10,479	14,800	2,806
(Other) Hardtop	N/A	N/A	N/A	28,496	40,930	25,754
Sedan Delivery	N/A	N/F	N/F	925	776	N/F
Same Deluxe	N/A	N/A	N/A	113	98	N/A
Ranchero 66A	21,027	20,937	20,842	12,218	9,916	10,539
Ranchero 66B	N/A	N/A	N/A	6,315	7,165	7,734
Ranchero 66G	N/A	N/A	N/A	N/A	N/A	16
Ranchero 66H	N/A	N/A	N/A	N/A	235	990

N/A Not Available

N/F Figures not available

From Ford Motor Company Production Records

Readers seeking Falcon Production details by Body Style are directed to "The Production Figure Book For U.S. Cars" by Jerry Heasley, presently available from the publisher, Motorbooks International, Box 2, Osceola, Wisconsin.

A 1965 Falcon Ranchero sits quietly awaiting its restoration on the Big Island of Hawaii in the Spring of 1982. Since "the Opera's not over 'till the Fat Lady sings", the Falcon story is not ended while these projects remain.

In 1964, recognising the value of organizing the typical enthusiastic Owners, Ford presented its Dealers with a complete Program for the formation of local Falcon Clubs. Included were a set of proposed Rules; instructions for setting up the Clubs; an interesting pamphlet describing for the prospective Members the enjoyment that they might expect to receive, and, above all, a folder advising the Dealer of benefits that he might expect to receive (added sales, increased service Department volume, etc).

Courtesy Charlie Jones, Obsolete Ford Parts, Nashville, Georgia

Readers seeking additional information on the subject may wish to consult the following:

Falcon Club of America
629 No. Hospital Drive
Jacksonville, Arkansas 72076

Ford Falcon Club of San Diego
P.O. Box 33306
San Diego, California 92103

Ford Falcon Club of Arizona
1515 West Hartford Avenue
Phoenix, Arizona 85023

The Ranchero Club
1339 Beverly Road
Port Vue, PA 15133

Parts Supppliers who may be of assistance:

Obsolete Ford Parts
311 Washington
Nashville, Georgia

Mike's Falcon Parts
4523 Toucan St.
Torrance, California

FALCON EDDIE
Jack Miller
2830 Belden Avenue
Hollywood, California 90068
213-463-0155